To:

Sue —

Dreams come true, but it's all up to you —

Just believe!

Love,
Elaine

D0615313

Create Your Own Fate

*Connect with Your Creativity
and Change Your Life*

Elaine Northrop

authorHOUSE®

AuthorHouse™
1663 Liberty Drive
Bloomington, IN 47403
www.authorhouse.com
Phone: 1-800-839-8640

First published by AuthorHouse 11/17/2011

ISBN: 978-1-4520-9185-3 (dj)
ISBN: 978-1-4520-9186-0 (sc)
ISBN: 978-1-4520-9187-7 (e)

Printed in the United States of America

Any people depicted in stock imagery provided by Thinkstock are models,
and such images are being used for illustrative purposes only.
Certain stock imagery © Thinkstock.

This book is printed on acid-free paper.

Dedications

To Sylvia Brown, the renowned psychic, who three years ago on a cruise ship told me I would write a book that would be very successful. Thank you, Sylvia, for reading my heart!

To Dr. Phil, whose show I tape every day and who has inspired me to want to write this book to help others.

To Howard Brinton, who asked me to join his group of Super Stars, which is where I first started teaching a course on Creative Visualization.

To my grandson, Jake, who took the time at age 13 to read my book and say that, just like on "American Idol", I was going to Hollywood.

To my super successful son, Creig, who is the embodiment of the principles in this book and is now the Number 1 real estate agent for all real estate companies in America. *I had a dream*, but my son's dreams were so much grander that he created a whole new level of success that I couldn't even envision. I applaud you, Creig, not only for the sensational son and the incredibly successful business man that you are, but for the father, husband, role model, and humanitarian that you have become. You have made me very proud and have provided me with a family to cherish from your wife, Carla, whom I love like a daughter, to your wonderful daughters, Kristen and Victoria, and sons, William and Jake. Together you make a sensational six-pack!

To my female best friend, Nicole, (who also happens to be my daughter) of whom I am so proud. Not only is she beautiful, but she is strong, sensitive, and successful—a great mother and wife. Although distance divides us physically, we are always close in thought and heart. She has found the perfect partner for her, a tall handsome Texan named Kevin, who has proved to be a fantastic husband and dedicated Dad. Together, they have produced two of the cutest and sweetest granddaughters ever, Katy and Haley, who continually bring much joy into my life. They bring out the little girl in me.

To my brother Bill, who has been there all of my life to live through most of this stuff with me. Thanks for being there for me when I needed you the most!

To our dear friends, Donna and Mario, who have served as sounding boards for my ideas and helped to guide my thoughts. Donna is also a successful author and has taken the time to edit my book. We love both of you and hope you will tour with us. You bring a lot of fun into our lives!

Last, but not least, to my darling Rick, the love of my life, my soul mate, (and what a dream mate he is!), my best friend, best buddy, best lover, and the best partner I could ever have throughout this life and into the next. I could not have had such an incredible fulfilling life if you were not in it to support me, console me, inspire me, and uplift me. I love sharing life with you and could not have written this book without you. How was I lucky enough to find the one man in this universe that was so perfect for me? He has also been a fabulous father for my kids as well as two daughters of his own—Rikki and Toni, and a grandfather to Nicolas. Rick, you have not only helped me to live this book; you have inspired me to write it, have contributed to it, and patiently typed it up for me (—many times). I adore you!

To all the people everywhere who will read this book and may get a glimmer of hope or an ounce of inspiration from it.......

Contents

In the Beginning......

This is not just another *rags- to-riches* story!

Although I grew up *poor*, I realized a long time ago that I have always been *rich* in the things that really matter— like love, family, and friends, which are the greatest riches of all. Instead, this is a story about learning how to create anything you want in your life, — first of all, by fantasizing about what you want and then by fabricating your fantasies into reality.

Since you cannot create outside of you what you cannot visualize inside of you, everything has to start in your mind. Once you learn how to manipulate your mind, you can create any riches you want either externally (by creating materialistic things) or internally (by creating happiness and joy). *Out of your dreams come desires, which motivate you to create and then to inspire!* When you follow these steps, you will enter the *Portal to Potential* and have unlimited access to fulfilling your fantasies and manifesting your dreams into your destiny.

This is also a story about the materialization of *me*, and how I became an *I*. Once I stopped being an object (a victim) and became a subject (an activator or creator), I learned to take control of my life and direct my dreams. My life hasn't been easy; but it has been a happy, fulfilling life, much more so after I learned how to visualize and materialize what I wanted in my life. Now I believe in *make-believe*, which is where it all begins.....

When I grew up in the 1940s and 50s, the man was supposed to be the *breadwinner* and the woman the *bread baker*. However, I experienced a real role reversal with my own parents. My mother had to go out and get a job to make the *bread* so we could have some *dough*. She actually provided a good role model for me as a provider.

My dad was a dreamer. His life was filled with an abundance of get-rich schemes, but there wasn't any real substance to any of them because he wasn't willing to work hard to make his dreams come true. My dad was a dreamer, not a doer. Being a gambler at heart, my father always thought that he was going to hit the jackpot one day or score big at the racetrack on a long shot. He loved gambling so much that most nights, after we kids went to bed, he would head to the local stag bar to play the nickel slots with nickels we needed for necessities. One Christmas, my mother even bought my father a slot machine to keep him at home; however, it wasn't the same to win his own money, so my father soon went back to the saloon. Sometimes he won, and we did actually become rich —for a day! When my father won, we got new toys and furniture. When he lost, we had a yard sale!

With a personality that could have sold snowballs to the Eskimos, my father should have been very successful at sales; but he just wasn't willing to apply himself. He sold just about everything (mostly door-to-door) including vacuum cleaners, Guardian Service Cookware, life insurance, and even Muntz TVs, until he ended up in real estate. His paychecks were sporadic and never amounted to much. Actually, what my father did best was play, either on his guitar or with us, which we children thought was wonderful. Happiness was my father's gift to the world. The gifts that he gave me were happy memories, a belief in myself, and unconditional love. You can't ask for much more than that!

Our family didn't have much money or any real security, but every year we managed to take a vacation on borrowed money. How I loved the ferry to Asbury Park with the five-cent *sodamats*, where you could get twenty different flavors by pushing all the buttons at once! I can still *smell that sea air*, as my mother would say when we got within twenty miles of the ocean! My mother never complained about money because she loved my father so much. The dichotomy of a player-father and a provider-mother was programmed in me at an early age. My parents lived a life of *outer scarcity* but always provided an *inner abundance* of love and happiness. While so many other parents offered their children a life of *outer abundance* but with *inner scarcity*. I knew I was lucky. I would choose an inner abundance of love, fun, and acceptance anytime.

My mother was thirty-five years old when she had me and (prior to my surprise) didn't think she could have any children. I think I knew *in-vitro*, when I chose Lew and Helene to be my parents, that what I wanted to do with my life was to spread joy and happiness. That's why I chose a happy-go-lucky father, who liked to play. However, I also knew I was going to have to learn responsibility in order to be able to raise a family on my own, so I chose a mother with responsibility— the perfect combination! My mother adored my father and never criticized him, even though her life was hard because of his constant desire to play. When my father played the guitar and sang at parties, everyone wanted to be around him. Everyone loved Lew! The rest just didn't matter! My brother turned out a lot like my dad—always jovial and looking for a good time. If I had my druthers, I would have chosen a jovial non-productive life too, and could have gone from being somebody's daughter to somebody's wife to somebody's mother. However, I may have never become somebody myself if fate hadn't intervened!

My dream when I was young was to become a teacher, although I didn't know how that would happen, as my parents certainly didn't make enough money to send me to college. Fortunately, fate stepped in. During my senior year of high school, when I was interviewing for academic scholarships, a mentor of my mom's died. I never had any grandparents, as they had all died before I was born; however, my grandmother's best friend took my mom under her wing when she became orphaned at an early age and periodically looked out for her. Aunt Minnie, who owned a department store in Washington, D.C., had no children of her own. When she died, she made sure she provided for my mom's children in her will, leaving each of us ten thousand dollars, a small fortune in those days! It was certainly enough to pay for four years of college at the University of Maryland,

and even to buy a car when I graduated—a baby blue Chrysler Imperial convertible. How I loved that car!

After I graduated from college, I taught English in high school for a year. I had been pinned to my first boyfriend from high school for five years, which lasted all through college, I thought I would end up marrying that man; but it wasn't to be. After we broke up, I craved adventure and decided I wanted to be an airline stewardess to see the world—that is, until I met my first husband. I met him at a bar one night when I got back in town fresh from airline stewardess school. He asked me to marry him the next night and I was foolish enough at twenty-three to say yes! In those days, you could not be a stewardess if you were married or even engaged. Since it was the middle of the year, I could not go back to teaching, so I took a job at Holiday Health Club selling memberships. That was supposed to be a temporary job, but I became so successful at selling that it lasted for eight years. I worked three twelve-hour days a week, which became difficult after I had two children.

However, my heart was always in teaching. I eventually returned to it for a while, until my world turned upside down. My husband of ten years ran off with a friend of mine, leaving me with no money and two small children to support on my own! All of a sudden I had to find something more lucrative than teaching to do for a living.

That is when I embarked upon a career in real estate, without actually having a clue as to what to do! It was ironic how I ended up in real estate, anyway. In those days, you didn't have to take a course to become a real estate agent. All you had to do was pass a test. I never really wanted a real estate license, but my ex-husband did. He had taken a three-month course and announced to me one Friday that he had to study all weekend to take the real estate exam on Monday morning. My husband suggested that I read his real estate book over the weekend and take the test with him on Monday. If I should happen to pass the test, I could then get a license. If I didn't pass, it wouldn't really matter, since I didn't want a license anyway. I read the book and took the test; but I prayed that if anyone passed that test, "Lord, let it be him!" I guess the Lord knew better, and the worse thing happened! I passed and he didn't, which was obviously a blow to his male ego and also to our marriage.

There I was with a real estate license that I didn't really want and didn't know what to do with. Little did I know how much I would need it later! In those days, there was no formal training on how to be a real estate agent. In fact, I couldn't even figure out what agents did all day except to wait for the phone to ring. And mine sure wasn't ringing! Since I had no name, no reputation, nor any track record or history of success in the real estate business, why would anybody want to buy a house from me? All I had was a *victim story* and two small children (ages six and four) who were dependent on me to be not only the breadwinner, but also their mother and *father*! However, my *victim story* (which I was sure would sell houses) didn't seem to be working, so I had to quickly figure out what else I could do. Little by little, I realized that my ex had no intention of supporting his children or me, and that there was very little I could do about it since he kept moving from state to state. My lawyers were always too late when they caught up with my ex and tried to garnish his wages because his bosses would tip him off and pay him in advance. After chasing my ex legally from state to state, which was getting me nowhere; I finally decided to stop and to concentrate on me.

I assessed my situation. I sure knew where the bottom was. I was there! Believe me, it was not a great place to be! I quickly decided that I needed to learn how to *create* my way to the top, as soon as I could see where the top was, by getting rid of the clouds!

Everything I have in my life now, I have created. Once I got in touch with the concept of *creative visualization* and stopped being a victim, my career took off. I ended up being Coldwell-Banker's number one international agent—a feat that I could not even have dreamed of accomplishing in the beginning! Furthermore, I was able to achieve that goal each year for three years—a record, that no other agent before me had managed to achieve. I was also asked to be a *Howard Brinton Superstar*, and was chosen as one of ten agents worldwide to be profiled in the book *The Millionaire Real Estate Agent*. All of this became possible because of my *conceiving and believing*.

I have now passed the baton on to my son, Creig, who because of his beliefs, has taken his dreams even higher. As the head of The Northrop Team, my son has expanded the business greatly to where he now has four offices in three counties (and over 60 team members). Last year, The Creig Northrop Team was ranked the *number one real estate team in America for all companies!* My son's dreams were bigger and broader than mine. After all, he had been spoon-fed a diet of *conceive, believe, achieve* since he was little. Needless to say, I am extremely proud of him!

I have also created the perfect partner for me, the love of my life and my husband of twenty-eight years, who stepped out of my dreams and into my life! *Oh, my God*, he even plays the guitar and can sing beautifully too! (Thank you, Dad!) I adore him, and together we have created a wonderful life. We designed and built our dream home, raised four kids, and purchased an oceanfront condominium in Ocean City. Everything I have in my life now—my success, my husband, my homes, my wonderful family—I visualized in my dreams first.

To give an example of how powerful this concept of creating whatever you want in your life is and how it works, I will tell you how I *created* our oceanfront condominium.

Twenty-five years ago, my new husband and I thought we were ready to purchase a second home *down the ocean* to enjoy some quality vacation time with the family. We had occasionally rented a unit on the first floor of a high-rise condominium, which actually overlooked the dumpsters and had a very limited ocean view. We loved the building though, because of its many amenities, like two pools and a tennis court. When the unit we had rented came up for sale at a price we thought we could afford, we made an offer to buy it. Before finalizing the offer though, I wanted to see everything else that was for sale in the same building—including an oceanfront penthouse (which I knew was way out of our price range!). However, once I saw the penthouse with its spectacular views, I knew I could never settle for less and had to create having a penthouse in my life. Since interest rates in those days were 16 to 19 percent, this was no easy feat.

My first thought was to look for partners—three other couples actually all said yes (until it was time to put up the money for the deposit.) When all three couples backed out, I was in a quandary.

I couldn't even imagine paying for the penthouse on our own. That thought was very scary because this unit was priced well beyond anything I believed we could afford at that time. However, in my mind, I kept visualizing my whole family having Thanksgiving dinner at the beautiful dining room table in this condo. My visions became so strong that I started believing that it could actually be possible. I felt I had to at least make an offer, so I made a low offer that was promptly turned down!

That was in September. I was really disappointed because I was so sure that my vision was going to come true, and we were running out of time to settle by Thanksgiving. Then I was crushed to learn that another offer on this penthouse had been accepted—a cash offer! I really started to question my beliefs and visions, which were so strong and positive. How could the universe have let this happen? It had let me down! *My psychic guides* quickly came back with a different answer though, by saying....

"Dummy, we presented you with the opportunity to create something wonderful in your life, but your beliefs weren't strong enough for you to make an acceptable offer. So you blew it."

I responded to those voices in my mind with *"Oh, my God, you are right. It was me!"*

My vision was right on, but my beliefs just weren't strong enough to make this vision happen. I begged the universe to please give me another chance to *believe* this vision into reality. What I was actually saying was, *"I need a miracle! This time I will make my beliefs strong enough to overcome my fears."* I prayed and kept visualizing, never giving up hope.

Several months later, I got a call from the seller's agent telling me that the cash buyer had disappeared, and his check had bounced! I knew this was my *miracle in the making*; and without hesitation, I pounced on the opportunity. I made a full price offer with a good deposit and asked the seller to do a wrap-around mortgage. My husband and I put up a hefty down payment and agreed to take over the payments on his mortgage, which were locked in at a 9% fixed rate. The offer was accepted! It was now January. We settled in March, and the next Thanksgiving, guess where we were with our entire family?

Once I *believed* that I could do it, the payment part actually became easy. I have never regretted this purchase for one moment, although I at first thought it was well beyond our means. My family and I have created many happy memories there. Beliefs *do* make things happen, but only when your belief and your desires become stronger than your fears.

Another lesson I learned from this experience is that there is no time in the universe. What I visualized as happening the year before actually happened a year later. I've had this happen many times with visualizations because they take some time to manifest. I actually visualized being Coldwell Banker's number one agent the year before that happened too. *Desires don't always arrive on schedule.* The important lesson here is *to never give up the belief that your visualizations will materialize when your desires become strong enough to believe them into being!*

Visualization has always been extremely important to me and has played a big part in my life. One of the visualizations I used in creating this book came from touring Italy and visiting the Sistine Chapel. Michelangelo depicted God giving Adam the spark of life through divine energy as their two fingertips barely touched. I envisioned that this would be how I would be inspired to write my book when the *Divine Source* sent its energy through me. I kept this image in my head and used it to write whenever the urge would strike. Every time *God gave me the finger*, so to speak, divine inspiration would flow through me. This book is the end result. It has taken me three years to write. I keep thinking of additional things that I want to include. But now, it is just time to say *Amen* and get this book into the hands of others who can hopefully benefit from it. *"Amen!"*

This book is about how to conceive and achieve whatever you want in your life by *believing* that it is possible. You see, if a thing or event that you really want to create weren't possible, you wouldn't be able to conceive of it in the first place. Once you can conceive of something that you really want to have in your life, it is the *belief* that it will happen that can take your life from *blah to bliss.*

Desire + Belief = Creativity

Wishing is a beginning
Wishing could also be the end
Wishing is not real,
But it could be….
When you wish your dreams into reality!

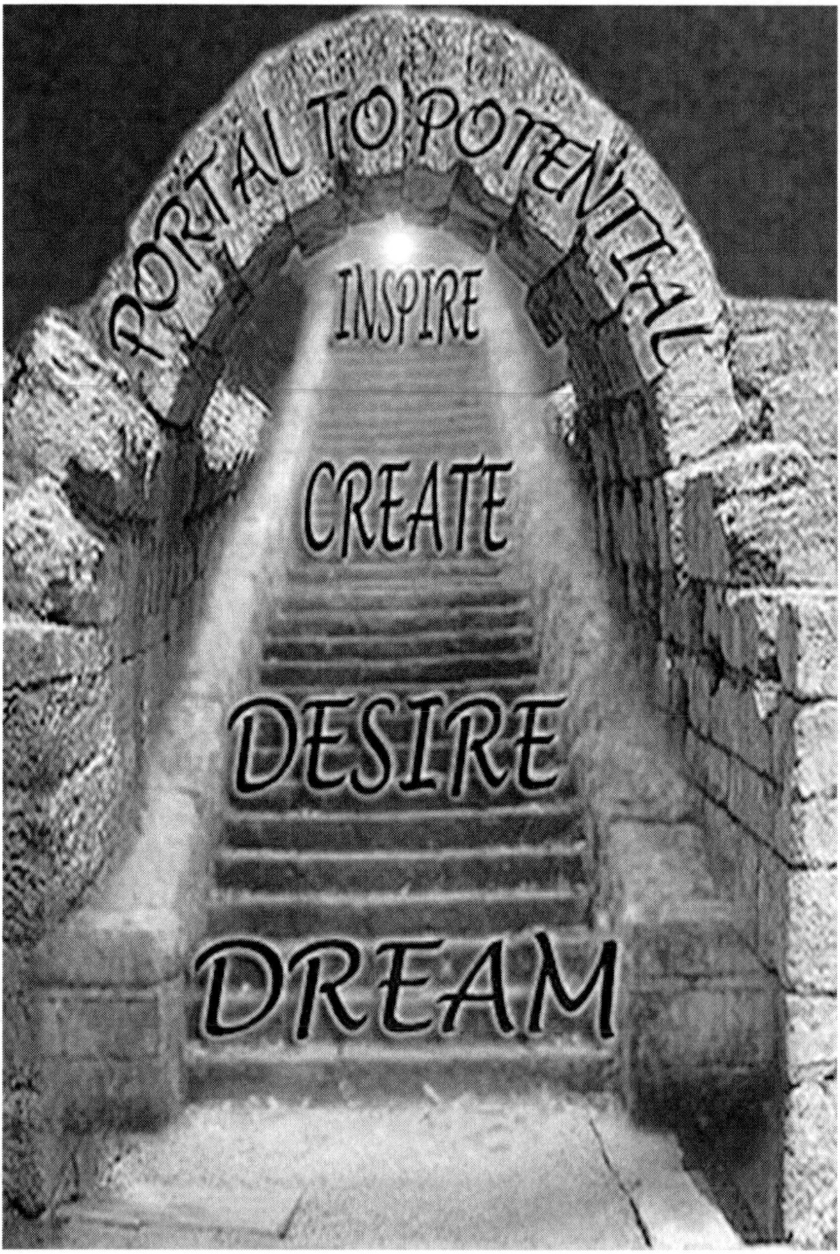
PORTAL TO POTENTIAL
INSPIRE
CREATE
DESIRE
DREAM

1

Conceive, Believe, Achieve

It is never too late to *create your own fate*! Your *life* is your *creation*; and consciously or unconsciously, you are recreating it every moment of every day.

Life isn't really about finding yourself. It's about *defining* yourself and creating the best you that you can possibly be. Then it's about learning how to celebrate yourself—the greatest creation that ever was!

The best way to predict the future is to create it! Your life can actually be anything you want it to be once you understand that you are in control of your life and are creating it moment by moment. Life indeed can be *magical*; but in order to have *magic*, there has to be a *magician*. You are the magician in your own life, creating illusion after illusion, all of which seem real, not only to the audience, but to you. Ironically, it is the *belief* that an illusion is real that transforms that illusion into reality.

Instead of living each day just to discover what it holds for you, wouldn't it be better to *create* each day the way you want it to be? Actually, you are creating your life every minute of every day anyway—probably without knowing it. When you finally get that you are in control of what happens to you, and that your thoughts are determining your future, moment by moment; you will choose better and create better. A thought originates within your imagination and then evolves through a process I call *creationalism,* which is the process of creating into reality whatever you are conceiving in your mind. This book is actually about creative visualization, or total transformation, but you can just think of it as *wishcraft. Wishcraft* is the art of manifesting your desires and wishes into reality. There is nothing evil about it. In fact, *wishcraft* can only work when you use positive energy and divine inspiration to craft your wishes into reality. Defining life just as a process of discovery and disillusionment denies the precious power that each of us possess to be, do, or have in our lives whatever we can imagine or desire. By connecting with our creativity and utilizing that precious power, we can bring prosperity, tranquility, and fulfillment into our lives.

According to God in *Conversations with God,* "The life process should be an experience of constant joy, continuous creation, everlasting expansion, and total fulfillment." The universe has given us the power to manifest anything we want. All we have to do is get in touch with that power. I could have called this book *Conversations with a Goddess,* but I'm not a goddess. I'm just an ordinary person, who has learned an extraordinary lesson—that when we are in touch with our heart's desire, we can manifest anything we want in our lives—as long as we *believe* that we can!

Having just come back from Disneyworld, I can think of no better example of how a fantasy in someone's imagination could inspire a billion dollar business! Maybe someone had conceived of a friendly mouse who could talk, sing, or walk before Walt Disney did; but no one else *believed it into being.* Imagination is incredible, but only when we can ignite our imagination and transform our thoughts into reality through our beliefs.

Our beliefs are the most important thing in our lives and the single most important factor in determining whether our dreams will come true. A long time ago, I adopted a magical mantra for my life which has dramatically changed the essence of my life. Garnering this phrase as a guide for my life, I now want to share it with the world. I have always lived my life with this conviction, "*If you can conceive it and believe it, you can achieve it;* but the most important thing is to *believe it!"*

Most people's thoughts go along the lines of *I'll believe it when I see it,* but the truth really is that *you'll see it when you do believe it,* and not before. Most things have to be believed to be seen. The most important thing about this concept is *the belief.* Most people are capable of conceiving things in their minds. That's called fantasizing. However, in order to make a fantasy materialize, you have to *believe it into being.* If you can create something in your mind and actually visualize that it exists, you can materialize it. When your beliefs become strong enough, whatever you see in your mind will actually create the world that you see.

Everything we have in our world now—our houses, every piece of furniture, every appliance that we own, our cars, and even airplanes all started out as someone's dream until those things were *believed* into reality. Actually you can *believe anything into being* if you believe hard enough and act as if that belief were already a reality. If someone hadn't *believed* the automobile into being, we'd all be hoofing it or riding horses. Nor would we be flying through the sky, or heating things instantly in a microwave had it not been for someone's vision and beliefs! We would all still be living in caves and cooking over an open fire if someone hadn't dreamed that life could be better. Even the thought of cooking over an open fire was someone's dream way back when.

As a matter of fact, fire came from man's desire—his desire to light the darkness, to provide warmth, and to cook his food. God provided the sticks, but man had to figure out what to do with them by using his imagination to create what he wanted. Fire was just one man's dream until he believed it into reality and then inspired others to use it. The wheel, the wagon, the chariot all started out as a thought or desire in someone's mind until that person actually believed it into reality.

The power of transforming a thought into something tangible exists in every one of us. An object can take one form until someone conceives of it as being something else. For instance, a rock would still be part of a rock pile if someone hadn't *conceived* it into being a cathedral. Life becomes magical when we can turn fantasy into fact!

Actually, *focus fabricates*, and anything that you picture repeatedly in your mind *replicates*. All it takes is the *belief* that it is possible!

Thoughts are constantly manifesting themselves into reality. Controlling our thoughts is the key to creating a new reality for ourselves. That control helps us make the choice as to whether we manifest miracles or misery in our lives. Once we understand that the choice is ours, why would anyone choose to manifest misery, when it's just as easy to manifest a miracle? Once you have grasped this concept, the next step is to take responsibility for creating your own life the way you want it to be.

Assess your life as it is right now. Take responsibility for having created it so far. That means you must take responsibility for all the good and all the bad things you have in your life. If you don't want bad things in your life (and no one does), get rid of them by blocking them out of your mind. You will find that the bad things will disappear the moment you let go of those unhappy thoughts. Likewise, when you own up to the responsibility for creating everything good that you now have in your life, you will realize that no one can ever take the good away from you. Since you created it in the first place, you can create it again if it should disappear. Once you are secure in the feeling that everything you have created so far can be created again, the fear of any material loss in your life is eliminated.

The famous philosopher Descartes once said, *"Je Suis, ergo sum,"* which means *I think, therefore I am.* I would change that to *As I think, I am* (but I can't say it in French!) Your mental pictures and beliefs about *who you are* are of paramount importance because *who you see is who you'll be!* Actually, the world that you see is the world that will be. Our background and circumstances have had an influence on who we were, but we are responsible for who we become. It's never too late to be who you might have been and live the ideal life that you visualize in your dreams. Unfortunately, though, most people become so busy just focusing on making a living that they don't have time to create a life! Don't get caught up in the *fog* of your daily routine and lose sight of the light!

As the continuous creator of your own universe, you are creating whatever you are feeling and thinking about in your life, moment by moment, day by day. Don't throw today away! If you want to be happy, start by feeling happy in the moment. There is always something to be happy about. Dwell on what makes you happy, and you will bring more and more happiness into your life as one happy moment succeeds another. You don't always get what you *want* in life, but you always get what you create. If you don't like the reality that is the result of your creation, it's because you are not focusing on what you want in your life. You are focusing on what you don't want and creating that instead. For instance, if you think your life is *the pits*, don't dwell on the pits. Think instead of the cherries that can be grown from those pits! Whatever your thoughts are conceiving is constantly materializing. Once you realize that your thoughts have the power to create, you have to learn to control your thoughts and confine them only to things that will bring you joy. Change your focus from a fear of failure to a future of fulfillment!

If you just think of *what is*, you're not changing anything. Think instead of *what could be*, and focus on that.

Remember, *unless* you change how you think, nothing will change. You will always have what you have right now because that is what your thoughts are creating for you each day. Your thoughts are so powerful that they actually create the forces that shape your destiny. Thoughts can propel you into prosperity, keep you stuck in stupidity, or worse yet, tie you up in tragedy. Don't focus on sickness or on your current problems, or you can't get anything to change. Focus instead on what you would like to have happen in your life. You can actually change your world by just changing your thinking.

Create the kind of life you would like to have in your mind first. Tell the story you want to live, and eventually you will live it. Focus on where you want to be, not on where you are Then move in the *direction of your desires*. However, you cannot create what you do not *believe* is possible. A person doesn't always get what they're looking for in life, but they do get what they *believe* they will find. So don't look for something without *expecting* to find it or *believing* that it will happen. If you want something different in your life, just *conceive* it and *believe* it. Then see yourself surrounded by the conditions you want to produce.

Don't block your bliss. Go to the source inside of you that generates happiness, and then believe that whatever you desire is already here! You can't *achieve* happiness, but you can *believe* happiness. The best way to get to happiness is to believe that you are already there.

Actually, *the quickest way to get anywhere is to believe you are already there*. But first, you have to know where *there* is. If you don't know where there is, you can run and run and never know when you reach the goalposts because you didn't set them up to begin with. That is indeed *the longest yard*, because you had no goal in mind but just kept running. How many of you are on a *treadmill of tedium?* "Round and round the mulberry bush, the monkey chased the weasel." Stop going round and round chasing a tail and go somewhere with your head!

Just think of yourself as a passenger getting on a private plane. Once you board the plane and take your seat, you can't expect the pilot to take off without any destination in mind. When you hire a private plane, the pilot will ask you where you want to go. In our subconscious, we all have an automatic pilot, who is constantly asking us, "Where do you want to go?" If you say, "I don't know", your pilot can't take off. If you say, "Oh, I just want to enjoy sitting on this beautiful plane eating peanuts and sipping wine," your inner pilot will remind you that this is a <u>plane</u>; and a plane, like your life, has a *purpose*, which is to *go somewhere*. If you just sit and do nothing, pretty soon the peanuts and wine will run out. Before that happens, your inner pilot will repeatedly keep asking you, "Where do you want to go?" If you keep saying "I don't know," you will go nowhere. Finally, your inner pilot, in frustration, will ask you, "Where do you picture yourself in your fantasies? What do you like to do?" If you give your pilot a clue, and at least say, "Well, I like warm weather," your pilot can take off and head somewhere south. However, your pilot can't land until you give him a more specific destination. That destination is determined by your desires and your mental pictures. What is it that you want, and where do you want to be? Further, when do you want to get there? If you picture an island in the Caribbean, that is a direction. But if you picture *yourself* at Bluebeard's Castle on St. Thomas island sipping a banana daiquiri at sunset, your pilot knows exactly where to take you and when to get you there. When you give your automatic pilot specific instructions, he can take you to the place where you want to go much faster—even before the peanuts run out! The more details you supply, the sooner you will get there.

If you have a *blue sky* dream and just say, "I want to see the world," that will never happen. Your dream has to be more specific, like "I want to go to Rome, Venice, and the Greek Isles this August." That is a dream that can be accomplished, because it has a specific goal and a time line.

Our hearts determine our dreams and desires, but our minds create those desires into reality through our beliefs and mental pictures. We each have within us the power to manifest anything we deeply desire. The map you need to get you where you want to go is your feelings. Where your pleasure is, your treasure is. Ask yourself, *"What is it that I feel passionate about?"* Then make your passion a priority. Get juiced and get going! Design your own mental map based on your passions. Passion is a feeling that is sparked by the love of doing something. Decide what turns you on. What makes your eyes light up with excitement when you talk about it? What makes your voice go up an octave? We all have catalysts that get us going. Go in the direction that your passion wants to take you, because any proposition without passion falls flat. Passion has power! Passion helps you to live a life of purpose.

The difference between passion and a goal is that passion is a *feeling* that gets you excited. A goal is what you want to achieve after you get excited. Figure out how to get paid for what you're passionate about, and you will be very successful indeed. Pursue your passion, and it will be a *pursuit of happiness*!

Unfortunately, most people plan their vacations with more thought than they plan their lives. Perhaps it's because escape is easier than change. We can design our lives with extreme care and get somewhere, or we can stay *stuck in sameness*—which is our comfort zone. (You know, that cozy cuddling with the couch!) The best way to get somewhere is to decide you're not going to stay where you are.

However, to leave where you are, you must first have a destination. If you don't have a destination in mind, how will you know when you have arrived? It's really very simple. You can't get *there* if you don't know where *there* is!

Actually, *there* is a different place for each individual. Decide where *there* is for you. See your destination clearly in your mind. Most people think in pictures. Everyone has a different picture of who they think they are and where they want to be. Place your mental picture on the top of a set of stairs so you can visualize what you want. It is not enough, though, to simply stare up the steps. You must also step up the stairs. As long as you can see the top, you know you are going in the right direction and will eventually get there, one step at a time.

Everything you will ever need to create the life you want is contained within you. Everything you need to know about how to succeed is already there inside of you. Search your soul. Whenever you are faced with a choice, pursue your passion. Choose what makes you feel good. Make that your goal in life. Focus on *I want to feel good.* (Why would you not want to feel good, anyway?) Create the life you want in your mind, and then it will materialize. Don't just create life as it *should be*. Be open to what *could be*. When you can find a state of nirvana inside of you that is not dependent on any other person, place, or thing, you have become the conscious creator of the state of mind that will enable you to find happiness in your universe. Your choices are as big as your dreams. Your dreams are as real as your ability to believe in them. You actually can have everything that you can conceive if you will just *believe!* Since we are creating ourselves anew in every moment of now, why not create *You*-topia? Take the *now* and create it into a *wow!* Let me show you how.

How can you create a clear mental picture of what you want and then make your dreams into reality? First of all, know that the most powerful thing in your life is *you*. Remember your thoughts create the forces that shape your destiny. Once you describe your life, you prescribe your life. So how does one write a prescription for happiness? All the forces of the universe are there ready to go to work for you to fulfill that prescription, but they're out of a job if you don't give them the prescription. Tell yourself, *I am a powerful, loving, creative person, and then write a prescription for what you would like your life to look like.*

Visualize what you desire *until* that desire becomes a reality. Visualize being in love with your world, and your world will love you. Actually, the more you give love to the world and receive love back, the more love you have to give. Be like a sponge, soaking up love and becoming softer and softer as you do. When someone squeezes you, love just pours out of you, and you can actually clean up any mess. Pursue your passions and let them help you create a new life that is in line with your divine design. How do you do that? First of all, align with your spirit. To be *inspired* means to be *in spirit*. Alignment with your soul's goals produces the power to create through your beliefs. Harness that power. Decide what your purpose is in life and pursue that purpose. Your purpose comes from the spirit inside of you. If you have a pulse, you have a purpose!

Spirituality comes from inside of you—from your spirit. There's a difference between religion and spirituality. Religion is a set of rules and beliefs that are imposed upon you by man-made sects. Religion is about rules. Spirituality is about feelings—feelings that come from inside of you. In order to be spiritual, all you have to do is go within, where your divine spirit exists. Since you speak the same language as your soul, you don't need an interpreter, rabbi, priest, preacher, or anyone else to intervene and tell you what you can or can't do. Everything you may need, might want to know, or may want to do is right there inside of you—including where you want to go in this life. Your soul knows the way. Since it came from the divine source, it can also find its way back to where it came from when it's time to return. In the meantime, you are in charge of the journey that your soul takes, where it goes, and what it wants to accomplish while it is here. Your soul is not lost. It doesn't need anyone else to show it the way, to pray for it, or worse yet, to pay money to buy its way back to its source. These are man-made tenets, which are intended to control your soul while it's here or your relatives when your soul has passed on. Take control of your own soul and trust that it knows what it is doing. Just believe that your spirit can actually create anything you want in your life.

Since we all are really *spiritual* beings inhabiting physical bodies, we have the power to produce anything from the spiritual world that we want and have it manifest in the physical world. Provided that it is good for us, everything that we want is just waiting for us to manifest it into reality. If that were not so, we could not even conceive of the thought that it was a possibility. Our physical bodies are just the housing or casing in which our soul resides. If we were just physical bodies, and nothing else, we would not have dreams or any belief that we could change our destinies. We would simply be buffeted around by circumstances like a bottle in the ocean. That would negate any purpose to our life. We are more than that!

We demonstrate our divinity every day by *dreaming*. But we must do more than just dream. Sometimes just the desire and belief are not enough. They have to be accompanied by action!

Dreams are like the stars in the sky. You can reach for them, but you can't touch them. However, if you follow them, they will lead you to your destiny.

*Now I wake me up to live
As I give life all I have to give!*

2

Creative Visualization Test

If you want to understand where you are right now in your life in terms of creative visualization, here is a short test that will define your current thinking. It is amazing how your answers will reveal the story of your life *as it is right now!*

To take the test, write your answers on a separate sheet of paper. Don't rely on your memory for the answers, because the answers are very important. Answer each question honestly. Be creative and elaborate. There are no right or wrong answers. It is simply your story.

The Test

1. Visualize in your mind that you are in a forest. Describe your forest.

2. There is path in the forest. Describe your path.

3. Along the path you find a cup. Describe your cup.

4. Further along, you find a key. Describe your key.

5. Next, you come to a brook. Describe your brook.

6. Then you come to a bear. Describe your bear.

7. Further along the path, you reach an obstacle. Describe your obstacle.

Interpreting Your Answers to the Creative Visualization Test

1 Your Forest

Your forest is your view of your life as it is right now. Your forest can vary from a bright, sunny forest to a dense, dark forest filled with weeds and underbrush. If your forest is a happy forest, where the sun can get through the trees and create a green lushness, you are happy where you are right now in you life. If it is a dark dense forest, where no light gets through; and, instead, it is filled with thorns, thistles, or underbrush, your view of your life currently is not a very happy one. Shining light, friendly animals, pretty flowers, and butterflies all make for a happy forest. Darkness, ferocious animals, denseness, thorns, or bramble bushes predict that your life is not very happy where you are right now—at least mentally. There is no right or wrong, good or bad forest. Your forest is just where you are choosing to live right now and shows how you view your life at the moment.

2 Your Path

Your path is your idea of where you are going in life. It can be a straight and narrow path or a winding path full of curves. The important thing is where your path leads. A path should lead *somewhere*. Those of you who see a destination at the end of your path, (particularly a happy one), know where you are going. A winding, curving path with no destination shows that you don't know where you're going in your life right now.

A straight, narrow path leading nowhere shows that you are afraid to deviate from what is expected of you by others because you're afraid of their criticism. Hopefully, you will get to your destination once you have determined where you want to go by visualizing that destination.

3 Your Cup

Your cup is your view of love. A silver chalice, a gold cup encrusted with gems, a fine piece of crystal or any priceless or valuable cup means that you value love. A disposable cup, a paper cup, or a tin cup shows that you don't value love very much right now in your life.

You should interact with your cup by drinking from it—partaking of love. Hopefully, you at least value your cup enough to take it with you. If you throw your cup away after drinking from it, you are having a *one-night stand* with your cup. The interpretation is that you don't value love or relationships currently in your life, seeing them only as something to be used and tossed away. As you drink from your cup, it should refill itself, spilling over with abundant love in your life that can never be used up. People who really value love take their cups with them and use them again and again. Their cups are very valuable to them, just as love is very important in their lives.

4 Your Key

Your key is your view of knowledge. The larger the key, the more you value knowledge. When you pick your key up and use it to unlock doors in your life, you know how important knowledge is, and believe that it is your *key* to the future. A skeleton key could mean that you will use knowledge to unlock skeletons in your closet. Even if you don't use your key immediately, you should take your key with you to unlock doors in the future.

To throw your key away or to ignore it means that you don't value knowledge very much at this point in your life.

5 Your Brook

Your brook is a symbol of your sensuality/sexuality. If you have an inviting, enticing brook that makes you want to get into it and get wet, you are a sensual person. An enticing brook is one that you can immerse yourself in completely. If you don't want to get all wet, you should at least get your feet wet. A babbling, gushing brook that you play in and enjoy shows you have a very healthy attitude toward sex. A lot of rocks in your brook that you perceive of as dangerous shows that you may be afraid of sex. Dirty mucky water that keeps you out of your brook means that you think sex is dirty. Washing something in your brook rather than just enjoying it is a very practical versus a sensuous view of sex, meaning that you will only use sex when necessary *to come clean.* Sitting on the sidelines near your brook, whether you're having a picnic, chasing frogs, or watching butterflies, means that you would rather enjoy sex vicariously than to be a participant. The best kind of brook is one that you can jump in, get wet, and enjoy!

6 Your Bear

Your bear represents your fears. A very large, ferocious bear that you can't get around shows you have a lot of fear in your life. If your bear stops you, chases you, or blocks you, it shows that you can't move forward because your fears are stronger than you are. If your bear eats you, it shows you are being consumed by fear. A soft cuddly bear that you can easily get around shows that you are in control of your fears. Although you respect your fears, you know that they cannot hold you back, because you know how to get around them. If your bear is a teddy bear, it shows that you have no fears and are very comfortable with being you and with whatever you want to do.

Notice in your story, whether you are controlling your fears (your bear) or they are controlling you! The size of your bear and your interaction with it tell the story.

7 Your Obstacle

Your obstacle is the thing that is currently stopping you from moving forward and doing what you want to do in your life. Your obstacle can be anything you visualize, either large or small. It's what you do with the obstacle that matters. If you recognize something as an obstacle, yet are able to move around it, your obstacle is not controlling you or keeping you from reaching your dreams. If your obstacle stops you dead in your tracks and becomes an obstruction, then you must find ways to remove the obstacle before you can move forward. Always remember that you are in control. *There ain't no mountain high enough* to keep you from getting what you want in life if you really believe in what you want.

When your answers are compiled, they comprise a true story. They tell the story of *you*, or at least where you are in your life right now. That doesn't mean you will be there forever. You can change your visualizations by changing your thinking. Your story is a great barometer of where you are right now. If you don't like the interpretation of your answers, at least admit that they are *you*, or where *you are right now*. There's nothing wrong with where *you* are right now unless it is where you don't want to be! Only you can make changes in your life and create a new story that reflects who you want to be in the future—a new you that you are happy with! Remember you can change your life for the better so that the new story you tell will be one that you like.

> *Just as you are the creator of your story,*
> *you are the creator of your life!*
> *It all starts in your mind....*

3

Making the Choice to Change

We're Off to See the Wizard! ....

How many of us wish there really was a wizard who could give us a heart, a brain, or the courage to free us from our fears? Well, the good news is that there really is a wizard within every one of us that can provide whatever gift we need as long as we *believe*. Accept your gift from the *wizard within* and then make *changes* in your life as if you already had that gift! How would you act if you already had everything you wanted or needed in your life? What changes would you make?

Change is inevitable. The seasons change, weather changes. Toddlers grow up, marry, and move away. We even change our clothes every day. Why then can't we change what we do not like about our lives? Why do we stay in a marriage that we are only tolerating because we don't want to be alone, or in a job that stymies us because we're afraid to grow? The *status quo* is a joke when everything else around us is always changing. *Life is transition.* Caterpillars become butterflies. Even the Earth revolves. It doesn't stand still. So why do we attempt to? If we know that we can't fall off of the Earth, especially when we are moving with it, what are we afraid of? Why do we tell ourselves not to make waves when waves may be the very thing that we need to carry us to the shore?

There are three change criteria that can manifest in our lives and indicate that a change is needed and should be executed.

People will instigate change when:

1. They hurt enough that they have to.
2. They learn enough that they want to.
3. They receive enough that they are able to

What will be the reason that causes you to change? Change is a choice—a choice that you can make whenever it becomes necessary. The important thing to realize is that you have the *choice*!

How much of your life is determined by choice, and how much is determined by circumstances? When you realize that you can't control your circumstances, but that you can control your choices about those circumstances, you can control your life. If you don't like the way your life is going, all you have to do is make better choices. That is how you *create your own fate*. Although you cannot choose your circumstances, you can choose your thoughts about those circumstances. If thoughts appear in your mind that are unwanted or unhappy, you can choose whether to accommodate those thoughts by giving them energy and power, thereby making them even stronger. Sometimes we let our minds get so overcrowded with thoughts of anxiety, fear, or guilt that we fail to remember that *Happiness Is Only One Thought Away!* Why keep happiness at bay? When we give excessive energy to the thoughts that do not make us happy, our minds are on overload and cannot manufacture miracles. Clear out the cobwebs and the clouds so that happy visions can come into the void.

The philosopher Immanuel Kant once said, "We see things not as *they are*, but as *we are*." Our mental filters actually change our reality into what we choose to focus on. Since we have the power to change our thoughts, we can actually change how things are!

When I get overwhelmed by things in my life, I use a visualization that my three year-old granddaughter taught me. She dressed up as Super Girl one Halloween, and still goes around saying, "I am Super Girl." When I am overburdened by work or the holidays; and the world is too much with me, I go around saying, "I am Super Girl". It helps! Nothing is too tough for me to tackle when I am *Super Girl!*

If you really want to make changes in your life and are looking for a wizard, you can *follow the yellow brick road* or call on the *WIZARD WITHIN* by utilizing the following steps to change your life.

The Eight Steps to a *New You* are:

Step 1– Dream!

Learn to dream while you are awake and set your intentions on having that dream come true. Since you have no control over the dreams that happen when you are asleep, learn to control the ones that happen while you are awake. Daydream! Decide what would make you happy in your life and dwell on it. Then create more of that in your life by visualizing about it every day. Be careful about what you think about, though, because you actually get what you are thinking about! Thoughts set up a jet stream of powerful emotions that determine our reality.

Listen to your emotions and don't be numb to your feelings. Feelings are the compass of the soul that will put you on the right course. Out of your feelings and desires, come dreams. Dare to dream, and then define those dreams in detail. As the old song says, "*You gotta have a dream. If you don't have a dream, how're you gonna have a dream come true?*"

Just as what you put into your body—whether it be food, alcohol, narcotics, or nicotine—determines what your body will look and feel like, what you put into your mind determines what your life will be like. Choose wisely. Envision only wholesome thoughts. Your thoughts become intentions, and those intentions become creations!

Remember, everything in life started out as somebody's dream. Never laugh at anyone else's dream. People who don't have dreams don't have much. Learn to live your own dream because if you're not living your own dream, you're living someone else's dream. Don't let that happen. Create your own dream.

The best thing you can be when you grow up is to be *yourself*. It takes courage to grow up and turn out to be who you truly are. *Be Younique!* Get in touch with your inner child, who loves life, and see what an ideal life looks like to you. When you think like a child looking forward to each day, you will design a life with plenty of play.

Find out who *you* really are. Don't define yourself as someone's spouse or parent. After all, you came to this planet to find *yourself*! Most of us, however, at the end of our lives, know more about everyone else than we do about ourselves. If that has happened to you, ask yourself, *"Where did I lose me?"*

Life is not about finding yourself. It's really about just being yourself. You don't need a compass to find yourself; you need a peeler to peel away the layers of who you're not. You know how when you're really looking hard for something, it always seems like you can't find it; then when you stop looking, it's right there in front of you! Life's like that. Stop looking on the outside for some image that you can put on that's not really you. Instead, look inside where the core of your joy and happiness resides. Then let that core create the real you!

Why doesn't everyone live the life of their dreams? Of course, you don't want your dream to come true if your dream is a nightmare! Dreams should be positive and happy. If yours aren't, then change your dreams before they do come true. Dreams are your version of what reality could look like. Why would anyone consciously create a negative dream? Yet how many people describe their lives as a nightmare? How many of those same people keep creating that same nightmare over and over, day after day? If you don't want to be in a hole, stop digging!

Make sure your dreams are positive before they do become a reality. The subconscious does not recognize the word *not*, so when you picture something that you do *not* want to have happen, guess what happens? Ask yourself "Why... *not?*" Don't let the *nots* that you are visualizing tie your life up in *knots*. When you picture something that you do *not* want to have in your life, that is exactly what you are creating.

Imagine if I said to you, "Try *not* to think of an orange orangutan sitting on the sofa next to you trying to put his arm around you, or a purple hippopotamus knocking on the door trying to get in because he's jealous." Guess what you would think about? Your subconscious did not hear the *not*. Why waste time thinking about what you do *not* want anyway? Instead, fill that space in your head with positive thoughts and create them into reality.

Step 2– Program Your Dreams As if They Were Already Reality

When you want to create something out of *nowhere*, believe that it is *NOW HERE!* The subconscious mind does not know the difference between reality and a dream, so if you program that dream into your subconscious as if it were already a reality, guess what? The subconscious mind will do everything it can to reprogram reality to conform to your dream.

What is reality, anyway? Isn't reality only an illusion—an illusion that is different for each one of us? It is really our perception of reality that determines our reality. However, we all have *selective* perception. Since our perception of reality is unique to each of us, whatever we *conceive* in our mind, we *perceive* as reality. In other words, you have to *fake it before you can make it*, and then you have to fake it until that fake is no longer fiction, but actually becomes fact. In our minds, it is the constant conceiving of dreams that are perceived as reality.

Picture a father singing a sentimental song over the phone to his wife and kids. The father has been away for a long time and is missing his family so much that, in his mind, he has created being home with them. His desire to be with his family is so strong that his mental picture becomes true because, in his mind, he's *"already there"*. Anything that you passionately want, fervently desire, and undeniably believe will come true if you can just perceive that you are *already there!*

Actually, if the essence of your dream weren't already real somewhere deep inside of you, you wouldn't be capable of having that dream. Listen to your dreams. They will sing a song that no one else can hear. Tune in to *your tune*, and let it change the *tone* of your life.

Step 3– Believe!

When you believe in something strongly enough, it *automagically* appears!

Beliefs are magical, especially when you add passion and desire to them. If you believe hard enough in something; it will come true, because like Peter Pan, you will create fairy dust to manifest what you believe in and want to have happen. When your dream does come true, if you want to give the credit to angels, fairies, leprechauns, Santa Claus, or the Easter Bunny, that is up to you. However, it is really your *beliefs that realign the reality in your life.* Take credit for the *magic* of your own beliefs, which actually create everything in your life.

The difference between a belief and a speculation is that a belief is a deeply held conviction that something is true. Speculations are intellectual, but beliefs are emotional. It's the emotion that makes the difference. Emotions create passion. Passion creates purpose. Purpose sets up intention that leads to action. Action creates results.

How do you decide what it is that you want out of life? Decide what you're passionate about. Determine what turns you on. What is it that makes your eyes light up, and your tail wag? Pursue your passion. Actually, you can have more degrees than a thermometer; but if you don't pursue what you're passionate about, you will never be successful. Passion gives your life purpose. Passion is a desire that drives us to express who we really are. Board that *Streetcar Named Desire*, and it will take you anywhere you want to go! Whatever you focus on and intensely want in your life will become a reality once you begin to believe that you are powerful enough to create whatever you want.

"Whatever lies behind us and even what lies before us are no match for what lies within us!" The most important belief is a belief in yourself. If you don't believe in yourself, no one else will either.

Enthusiasm is the greatest asset anyone can have and the key ingredient to success. Enthusiasm excites energy! Start a momentum in your life by focusing on something that you really want. Feel it passionately in your own heart, then share it with others around you enthusiastically— Enthusiasm is contagious!

You orchestrate what happens to you in your own life. Although others may play the instruments, you are the conductor. If you don't like the music your life is making, select another tune—one that has oomph and fire!

Step 4— Set Goals

Goals are dreams with a deadline! A timeline is the difference between a dream and a goal. Before you take off and head in the direction of your dreams, you should have an ETA (estimated time of arrival). By the way, *someday* is not a day of the week!

Goals should be specific. Don't just say, "I want to do better." You have to name it to claim it. Give your goal a picture, a face, and a place. Decide on the deadline by which you want to achieve that goal. Say, "I will make "X" amount of dollars by August," or "I will write my book and have it published by June." Do a reality check on your goals periodically. In January, have you achieved one-eighth if your goal? In April, are you halfway there? If not, you need to step up efforts, or you will not make your deadline. Perhaps you need to put more pressure on yourself to achieve those goals. After all, pressure is what turns rough stones into diamonds!

Also learn to set your goals as *floors* and not *ceilings*. Set your goal as the absolute minimum you will achieve, but always give yourself permission to go higher. When I first started setting goals, I found that I was constantly achieving my goal; but, somehow, I never exceeded my goal. Then I realized that I was actually limited by my goals, as grandiose as I thought they were! My goal had become my *glass ceiling*. I could see beyond that ceiling, but could not get beyond it until I changed my beliefs. Now my goals have a floor but no ceiling because I have learned to eliminate my limits!

I remember the moment that happened for me in real estate. I was at a seminar many years ago given by a very knowledgeable speaker, Howard Brinton. At the time, I was probably the most successful agent in the room and was right on track to achieve my goal that year, which was five hundred thousand dollars in gross commission income (C.G.I.), before the split with my broker. I was feeling pretty good about myself, but really listened as the speaker said, "See your goal clearly in your mind. Really focus on your present goal. Then *double* that goal!"

My mind went crazy! I could not conceive of producing one million dollars in G.C.I. After all, I was already working too many hours! The left side of my brain kept saying, "No it's not possible! There are only so many hours in a day!" However, the right side of my brain started saying, "Why not?" and "If not *you*, then *who?*"

Thank God, I leaned to the right, and it was the right move. Once I could conceive of a new goal and started believing in it, I achieved it. Nothing had changed, except my thinking and my beliefs. In reality, I didn't work any more hours or any harder. I just worked smarter, started building a team, and never after that fell below one million dollars in G.C.I.—my new floor! I also gave myself permission to go higher (which I often did) because I set no ceiling. I thought to myself, *Why not go as far as I can with my new limitless beliefs?* With that attitude, I consistently set new records and was Coldwell Banker's number one international agent for three years—quite a feat in those days. I did it all because of my beliefs!

When setting goals, make sure to set a goal that is within your control. You cannot control the weather or other people. To say that your goal is to have a white Christmas can be very disappointing when the weather doesn't cooperate. But if your goal is to have an old-fashioned Currier & Ives kind of Christmas, that you can control. Don't set a goal for a specific person to fall in love with you, but you can set a goal that the *perfect partner* for you will come into your life within two years. Don't set a specific goal that Mr. and Mrs. Smith will buy a house that you have listed on Mayfield Ave. Visualize that the perfect buyer for your listing on Mayfield Avenue will come along within a month. That way you are not controlling others. You are only concentrating on achieving your own goals. Then your goals can materialize because they are not dependent upon any other person's behavior—only your own.

Sometimes you must attempt the impossible to know what is possible. The floor of your goal should be high enough to challenge you, but attainable with effort, so that you will feel good when you reach your goal. Always give yourself permission to go higher. Make sure your sky has no ceiling. Your income is only fixed if your thinking is fixed. What a shame it would be if your income grew, and you didn't!

After all, we are not just human beings. We are human *becomings.* The road to success is always *under construction.* Focus on where you want to go, and you will create the quickest way to get there as you set pavers in your mind. When you focus on the destination, the road will actually pave itself. However, if you're on the *road to nowhere* because you can't visualize a destination, you'd better make some changes quickly!

Anything worth having in your life is worth working for. Don't just say, "I want it all now!" People who expect instant gratification like a two-year-old are destined for disappointment. Children have great expectations and are disappointed when they don't materialize right away. Although we have the power to manifest anything we ardently desire, there is no such thing as *instant manifestation.* It takes time to create a magnificent masterpiece. Maturity is knowing how to control your expectations in order to mold them into reality and to accept what you cannot change. People who have tenacity and patience understand that achieving what they want is a process. As one small success succeeds another, these people keep heading in the right direction because they have chosen action over inertia. If these people make a mistake, they will realize it was their mistake, correct it, and move on. On the other hand, people who blame others and who believe that it is the world that needs to change and not them, live in resentment while they're waiting for the world to change, which never happens.

It is not your job to change the universe. (Who put you in charge of it in the first place?) It's your job to change *you* so that you can get where you want to go from where you are right now. If you're attempting a journey of a thousand miles, it would take you a long time to get there by foot; but you could take a bus, train, or plane and get there faster. It all starts with visualizing where you want to go and taking the first step in the right direction, even if it is just a baby step.

Your mind is like a built-in navigation system. It knows where you are without your having to tell it. What it doesn't know is where you want to go. You have to program in the destination, and the universe will figure out the details. Once you have decided where you want to go, try believing that you are *already there*. That is always the fastest way to get anywhere!

Whatever you focus on, your brain will automatically take you to. You need only to create the target and make sure it is always in sight. Remember it is almost impossible to hit a target that you can't see or one that is constantly moving. Have *target fixation* on a permanent target, (something that you really want). That way you will always stay on target.

Decide on your destination, and let that determine your destiny. Always head in the direction you want to go in by focusing on your destination. Don't look back at where you've been or stay where you are if that is not where you want to be. For instance, if you're leaving Baltimore and San Diego is your destination, don't stop in Dallas and say, "I'll never get there!" Focus on San Diego *until* you get there.

There's an old saying, *Build your castles in the air. That's where they should be. Then go out and put foundations under them.* Create castles. Believe them into reality, and you will live like a king as you design your own destiny!

Once you have your game plan and know what you want to create, enroll and enlist others to empower you in creating what you need. *The world steps aside for anyone who knows where he is going!* Surround yourself with people who want you to succeed. Don't hang out with people who are where you don't want to be. If other people are going nowhere, leave them there. Don't catch their contagious condition of complacency. Have you ever heard the old saying, *If you lay down with dogs, you'll wake up with fleas?*

Leave the dogs behind scratching their heads, wondering where you went, and how you got there!

Step 5– Study Success

Study your successes and those of others who have gone where you want to go.

Use people who are more successful than you as your role models. Pick their brains. Emulate what you think made them so successful. I know that when I was just starting in real estate, I looked at who was at the top and tried to figure out why. There was a woman in my office whose success in sales had catapulted her into being the top agent. I tried to figure out the secret to her success. The secret was certainly not in her looks, her personality, or her vitality. She even walked with a limp, which had to make it painful for her to show houses. What then was her secret? The only thing she did differently than anyone else was advertising—lots of it! In a day when agents relied upon the broker to pay for advertising (which was always in the broker's name), this woman was spending her own money to advertise her own name. Everyone thought she was crazy, but not I! Taking a page from her book, I started to advertise as much as I could afford. Not only did I advertise my name, but I also advertised my listings. I even went a step further and wrote creative stories about my listings, giving each house a name and a little story. My ads became famous. For example, I called one house "Cinderella" and wrote, "Someone waved a magic wand and turned this rather ordinary home into a raving beauty. See it before the 'stroke of midnight,' or it will be too late!" Or, "This home has a heart! To see it, follow the yellow brick road or call the wizard, Elaine Northrop." About a split foyer home, I wrote "Finally, a split with personality!" The public loved my ads, which were actually much longer than the above examples. My marketing created a stir in the marketplace. Pretty soon, many sellers were calling me because they wanted me to list their home, just to have me write a story about it. The more money I made, the more I invested back in advertising, which really paid off for me. Subsequently, I became the number one agent in my office, and the rest is history.

Utilize the concept of *niche marketing*. Find your niche and make it *U-nique*! In other words, get a gimmick. "If you're going to bump it, bump it with a trumpet!" Don't just sell real estate, specialize in something like old historic homes, high-end homes, lots, condos, or even in a particular area. Be the best in that genre and the only one to call. Use *tip-of-the-tongue* advertizing to be on the top of everyone's list when they think of your specialty.

Relish your own successes. Dwell on those successes and not on your failures. For every house that didn't sell, I had five that did. I publicized only the ones that sold. Success propagates success, but give success *an address* so you will know when you have arrived. That address will let you know when you are *home*. Remember, success only comes in cans — not can'ts!

Step 6– Remove the Blocks

Everyone has hurdles in life, but not everyone realizes that hurdles are for jumping over and not huddling behind. Keep in mind that the things that upset you can also inspire you. When you are feeling negative about anything, discharge that energy immediately. You can actually inhibit yourself or inspire yourself with your mental pictures. Don't think about what you don't want, or you run the risk of creating exactly what you don't want since your subconscious cannot interpret what you are picturing mentally. The subconscious believes that your thoughts should be transformed into reality, so it creates whatever it is that you are picturing and dwelling upon. Your life in the moment is what you're creating it to be; and, hopefully, it is based on what you want it to be. Don't let hurdles stop you when they're actually nothing more than speed bumps. Recognize however that the hurdles are there for some reason, even if it's just to get you to slow down and enjoy the scenery. Ask yourself, *How can I get over this hurdle?* or *What am I supposed to learn from it?* Then move on. Remember that you are in control. According to Vince Lombardi, "Obstacles are what we see when we take our eyes off the goal."

THERE ARE NO ACCIDENTS IN THE UNIVERSE. Everything happens for a reason. If you are on the right path, everything in the universe seems to fall into place as a sign that you are meant to go in that direction. When you are going in the wrong direction, roadblocks and obstacles will appear as signs to get your attention. Stop and ask yourself, *Why is this road so difficult? Is there a better way for me to go so I can move on to my divine destiny, which should be an undeterred destination?*

Sometimes when you're going down the wrong path, the universe will place obstacles in your way. It is up to you whether you view that obstacle as an *obstacle* or as an *obstruction*. An obstacle can be gotten around. You can bypass it, surmount it, or remove it so that it becomes nothing more than a temporary detour in your life. An obstruction stops you dead in your tracks and keeps you stuck where you are. You are the one who decides whether something is an obstacle or an obstruction through your beliefs and your interpretations. Sometimes when you decide to surmount an obstacle, the view is much clearer from the top, and the path is all downhill from there. Don't let your obstacle stop you, although it may temporarily block your view. Ask, *What am I to learn from this obstacle?* and move on. Don't turn your obstacle into an obstruction. Whatever your problem was yesterday, turn it into a challenge today. Just have faith that the *power* that is within you is greater than the *problem* that is in front of you.

After all, you are not who you were yesterday. You become what you *do*, not what you *did*. Problems are just divine opportunities in disguise. Yesterday's problems are actually today's opportunities to make a new decision. There's an old saying that *the reason most people don't recognize opportunity when it knocks is that it often comes disguised as misfortune.* Some people won't even open the door to opportunity because of their fear of what's on the other side. Don't let your fears keep you from fulfillment. If the universe puts rocks in your path, use them as stepping stones to get where you're going.

View obstacles as opportunities. An obstacle is objective. It is just there. It's your interpretation of that obstacle that makes it into a constant irritation, a disaster, or just simply fertilizer that may be unpleasant to deal with but produces beautiful blooms. Observe your obstacle. Don't run from it or let it stop you. Figure out how to turn your obstacle into a stepladder to help you rise higher so you can better see the purpose for which it was intended.

There's a story about a farmer and his donkey that illustrates this point. A farmer had a donkey, whom he was very fond of. As he got older though, the donkey slowed down because of pain and could no longer do the work that the farmer needed him to do. One day the donkey accidentally fell into an old well that was defunct and should have been filled in. The farmer, who would have never had the heart to get rid of the donkey otherwise, thought he could solve two problems simultaneously. By filling in the non-functioning well with dirt, the farmer thought he could bury the donkey, thereby relieving him of his pain. The farmer got a shovel and started to throw shovelfuls of dirt and manure over the donkey.

The donkey (who never dreamed that the farmer was trying to kill him) shook the dirt off his back and used each shovelful of manure to step on. As the farmer kept shoveling more and more dirt into the well, the donkey thought the farmer was actually trying to help him. *Shaking off the shit*, the donkey climbed higher and higher on the dirt pile, using each shovelful of adversity to advance. When the donkey finally got to the top and could actually step out, the farmer was really glad to see the donkey. He realized how smart the donkey had been to get to the top and let the donkey live until he died a natural death. The poor old donkey never knew that the farmer wanted to kill him because he didn't view the farmer's actions as adversarial. Instead, he thought the farmer was assisting him. The donkey remained happy because he used his obstacle as an opportunity. What does a dumb donkey know that we could all learn a lesson from?

Whenever manure gets piled on top of you, shake it off, and step on top of it! Life is going to shovel shit on you—all kinds of shit! The trick to getting out of the well is to shake off the shit and to use it as a stepping stone. All of our troubles are really just stepping stones. We can get out of the deepest wells by utilizing those stepping stones. Never give up! *Shake off the shit and step up!*

Use your adversities to advance! Let them make you stronger, and then use those adversities to your advantage as you rise to the top. Always remember the three A's—**A**ttitude **A**bout **A**dversity. It's your *Attitude About Adversity* that will cause you to advance or to retreat in defeat.

There is another way to remove an obstacle or a thought that is bothering you, and that is by using visualization. In your mind, create a huge silver ball that is coming to you from the universe. When the ball gets close, open it and put whatever person or thing that is bothering you inside. Anything negative belongs in that ball. Now close the ball, and hurl it back into the universe. See it becoming smaller and smaller the further away it goes. Finally, the ball becomes so small that it turns into a ragweed on a stem. Hold that stem and blow the feathers away, letting the universe deal with the particles so that they no longer bother you.

Never let a negative thought stay in your mind and fester, as it will only pollute your mind. Like a bullfighter, dance with doubt. If doubt attacks you or if someone is charging at you in anger, step aside and hold out your cape so that the thrust of the bull goes into the cape and cannot harm you. Keep side-stepping with your cape, and you will never be hurt by doubt or anyone else's anger.

Since our minds are capable of thinking only one thought at a time, negative thoughts can actually block out positive thoughts taking up the space that could be used to produce much better results.

Stay away from people who are *energy vampires* and suck your positive energy, leaving only negative thoughts in the void.

Resolve any resentment and release it before it festers. Allowing yourself to feel resentment toward someone is like letting someone you don't even like live in your head *rent free*. While that person is there, no one else can move in, although a tenant that you like would bring you much better returns. Evict the felon, and let good thoughts move in. If you continue to live with resentment and seek revenge, you actually dig two graves—the other person's and yours. Anger sends out darts to your own heart. If someone has hurt you, plug the hole in your soul. Walk away and let the wounds heal, or you will continue to bleed. When you feel that things couldn't get any worse, act relieved. Know that any improvement then is for the better. Remember, even when you're down to nothing, you can always rest assured that God is up to something! Sometimes God just needs to clear the clutter in your life so that you can see clearly.

As long as you entertain the thought that there is something or someone else out there doing something to you that hurts you, you are choosing to be a victim. Victims feel powerless because they have given their power away and are actually under someone else's control. When you lament about someone doing something to you that you do not like, you are actually giving control to that other person. Step back for a moment and realize that you are in control, not of that other person's action, but of your *reaction*.

It's all about how you perceive yourself. There are actually two ways that you can perceive of yourself—as an "*I*" or as a "*me*". An "*I*" is always the subject of a sentence and causes things to happen. A "*me*" is the object to whom things happen. The *me's* really have no control over what happens to them, since they are an object or *victim* in life. Things are always happening *to* or *for* them over which they have no control. Monitor the *me* in your life. Be proactive instead of reactive. Become the cause and not the effect by taking control. Only when you can say, *I created this*, can you take back the power to change it. When you start to move your "*I*" in a positive direction, slowly but surely, you will see changes happen. Don't feel insignificant or powerless to change anything. Remember, no snowflake in a snowstorm ever felt responsible for having caused a blizzard! Just move in the right direction, and positive energy will follow.

If you don't take responsibility for your own behavior, you can't change the consequences of that behavior. Having chosen a consequence because you chose the behavior is the same thing as having created it. It is only when you can accept responsibility for all of something that you can change the part that is in your control.

Events, occurrences, happenings, and circumstances are all created out of your consciousness. Why then do you create what you do not want? An event is just an event, but your interpretation of that event is *self-invented*. Events are emotionally neutral but an event becomes good or bad depending on your interpretation of it. Sometimes an event can be the universe's way of causing you to go in a different direction, which might actually be much better for you. In reacting to a particular event, you can rebel or recoil, which will cause you to live with the repercussions; or you can simply accept the event and look for the lesson that goes with it. Accept *what is*, but always ask *what if*!

Whenever something happens over which you think you have no control, you still have the choice to act or to react. If you react with anger or fear, you are setting yourself up for more negatives to come your way. Accepting an outcome and being at peace with it doesn't mean that everything is perfect. It just means that you have decided to see beyond the imperfections by looking for the good in any situation and taking total conscious control of your thoughts and actions. By reacting to your interpretation of a situation instead of just accepting that situation the way it is, you can actually block a positive outcome in your own mind. Many of us choose to think negatively about something that we really do want just so that we're not disappointed when it doesn't happen. We're afraid to hope and think positively because we don't want to set ourselves up for a letdown. The trouble is that our subconscious mind is trying to match the mental pictures that we program into it. Since the subconscious cannot censor our thoughts, the subconscious creates what it thinks the conscious mind wants. Ironically, when you think negatively to avoid disappointment, you are actually creating the negative result that you didn't want! Never program negative thoughts into your subconscious. Even if you say to your subconscious, *"I will <u>not</u> fail"*, all the subconscious hears is the word *fail*; and that is what it will create. Instead, plant the thought, *"I will succeed"*; and you will!

Our thinking is of paramount importance. Sometimes, we don't recognize help when it is being given to us, because it may not come in just the way we want it to. Take, for example, the story of a fisherman, who is sitting in his rowboat, when, all of a sudden, his boat develops a leak. A neighboring boat, noticing that the fisherman is in trouble, comes over to try to help him. The fisherman, however, refuses the help, saying that "God will save me." A second boat also notices that the fisherman is in trouble and calls the Coast Guard, who come to rescue him. Again, the fisherman refuses their help, insisting that "God will save me" (even though at this point his boat is half full of water!). The Coast Guard puts out a distress signal; and a helicopter arrives with a rope ladder and a megaphone, pleading with the fisherman to grab the handle and be saved. Foolishly, the fisherman again refuses their help. As his boat is going down, the surprised fisherman mutters with his last breath, "God, I trusted you and surely thought you would have saved me! Why have you forsaken me?" Loud and clear, God's voice comes back to the fisherman, "But I didn't forsake you, my son. I sent the first boat, the Coast Guard, and the helicopter. When you refused all of that help, I just thought you wanted to drown!"

Just like the fisherman, how many people in life take no responsibility to help themselves to create their own future? Instead these people take the attitude of *que sera, sera* (whatever will be, will be). On the contrary, I have always maintained that if it's meant to be, *it's up to God and me*! God sends help, but we have to show how badly we want something by taking positive action on our own. God does his part, but we have to take part and do our part too, by recognizing that help and grabbing hold!

When you realize that you are the creative power in command of your own circumstances, you become the master of your own fate. By taking control of your own life, you can create your own happiness. However, taking control can sometimes be frightening because, with that control, comes responsibility. We can't really blame others for our reality if we are in control of it and realize that we have created it. As long as we blame someone else anyway, whether it be our parents, our husbands, our children, or our bosses for whatever happens to us, we are actually giving our power away. Blame creates anger and negative energy. It implies that you have passed your power on to someone else. Maybe that is why you feel so drained when you become angry. When you blame someone else for your unhappiness, it implies that someone else is in control of your happiness and, therefore, of you and your life.

Take your power back by controlling your own thoughts rather than letting those thoughts control you.

Break out of the *prison of your past*! Don't let your past become your future by continuously repeating past behaviors and patterns. Actually, the one thing that we are powerless over is the past. We cannot change it. All we can do is accept it or regret it. If we choose to regret or resent our past, we are letting that past block out our new dreams. Don't let your *history haunt you*. You can't fix your past by criticizing others who have hurt you, but you can fix your life by setting goals for yourself and having a positive plan for your future. *Rise above your raising* by not judging others. Judging others doesn't really change the person you are judging. It changes you because it puts negative thoughts in your mind. When you judge people, you don't have time to love them. Instead of playing the *blame game*, aim for understanding and love.

It's important to have empathy for others, who may say to you *"walk a mile in my shoes"*, which is their way of asking for your understanding. Take time to be sympathetic toward someone going through a crisis, but eliminate constant energy drains. When you are constantly being pulled outside of yourself by the needs of others, you are externally focused. If your own *shoes* don't fit, are too tight, and pinch or hurt your feet, then change them. When others see you walking happily in your *new shoes*, perhaps they will change theirs. Remember, you didn't pick that other person's *shoes* for them, and only that person can decide to change their *shoes* if their feet hurt. All you can do is set a good example for them. Your job is to be awake to being alive, and not to host *pity parties* for yourself or others.

Do a reality check on your life right now. Ask, *Am I really happy? If not, why not? What is stopping me from being truly happy? What is it that I want out of life, and what changes am I willing to make to get what I want?*

Take time to think about your life before time takes you. Since there is no expiration date on anyone (at least I've looked and looked and can't find one on me!), we never know which day will be our last. If we did know, would we not want to spend that last day in joy, happiness, and total love for everyone? Since we don't know which day will be our last, why not spend every day that way—just in case!

There is actually good news and bad news for all of us. The good news is that you created your life and are responsible for it. The bad news is that you created your life and are responsible for it. Since you are responsible for your life either way, that also means that you can change your life. But only *you* can change your life— if and when you're ready to. How do you change your life? — *By changing your thoughts.* The outer world of circumstances will shape itself to the inner world of your thoughts. You cannot choose your circumstances, but by choosing how you react to those circumstances you can indirectly shape your destiny.

The first step in changing anything is to acknowledge the responsibility for having created it in the first place. When unfortunate things do happen (and they will) remember that you chose those things to be in your life for some reason. If a tragedy happens, don't think of it as a misfortune or of yourself as a bad creator. Your mistake was not in choosing those uncomfortable circumstances, but in labeling them as bad since you chose them. Ask yourself, *Why did I create this thing in my life, and what am I supposed to learn from this experience?* Once you understand better, you will create better. Just know that each experience that you chose was necessary in order to gain that understanding. When you get in touch with your divine self (who you really are), your choices will be much better. As a result, your creations will be much better as you become more aligned with who you are and what you really want out of life. When you look at life in this way, all experiences, good or bad, actually serve a purpose. Life can show up for you in no other way than the way in which you think it will, since you are the one who thought it into being in the first place..

Whether you look at life through a telescope or a microscope, the view is awesome *if* you can see clearly without anything blocking your view.

Step 7– Remake Your World

Be aware that this is a universe of illusion. Become an illusionist, but don't let your illusions limit you. Since your mind can place you in a pasture or a prison, it is actually up to you to decide where you would rather live. Life is all a matter of perspective. If your current life is not working for you, it is up to you to do something about it. To create a new reality in your life, it may be necessary to change your thinking. Sometimes all you have to do is change *your mind about yourself!* Just as when you change your clothes, you will look different. When you change your mind, the world will look different. Take stock of your life. Do you like where you are right now or what life is showing you? If you don't like where you are, *move or make changes. You're not a tree!*

Remember, God didn't promise you a rose garden; but he did supply you with enough dirt and seeds to grow one if you wanted to. The planting, nurturing, watering, and pruning are up to you. You can grow just weeds or beautiful roses in your garden, but the desire and nurturing have to come from you. How is your garden growing? Are you making the effort to create beautiful blooms, or are you growing only weeds? To be a great gardener, the first thing you must do is picture the blossoms in your mind before they appear. Then you have to go out and do the planting, weeding, and watering. The universe will take care of the rest!

It's the same way with your life. Are the blooms that you are producing what you want them to be? Are they worth picking and savoring? If not, create a lifestyle makeover right now by attempting to align your reality with your dreams. Decide what you really want in your life, and then remodel your life so that it reflects what you want. Your world is actually a mirror of your mind. Do you like what you're seeing in that mirror? If not, don't delay happiness so long that you forget what makes you happy! Instead—create a reality that is in line with your dreams.

There are actually *three* steps to creating a new reality in your life!

1. Define what you desire. Make your definition short and to the point.
2. Wish for that desire in the present tense (as if it were already here) and then act as if it were.
3. Make your desire unlimited, thereby creating an abundance of anything you want in your life.

Once you have grasped these principles for creating what you desire, you can advance confidently in the direction of your dreams!

Step 8– Replace Doubt with Desire

When you desire something strongly enough, all doubt in your mind about having that desire should be dissolved. Our hearts determine our desires. Our heads program those desires into our destiny. What do you desire? Can you focus on your desire with such determination that it becomes a reality in your life? It takes concentration and perseverance, but whatever you fervently desire can become a reality.

Think about how you picture your life. Events in your life can happen either *for you* or *to you*, depending on how you interpret an event. If things happen *for you*, you say that they are opportunities. If things happen *to you*, you become a victim; but only because you choose to be! The difference is in your attitude about what happens. Remember, an obstacle can also be viewed as an opportunity. Deciding whether something is an opportunity or an obstacle is actually up to you. Give yourself a green light to enjoy your life, knowing that you do not create all the events in your life; but you do create the extent to which an event *touches* your life. The way to reduce the pain in any experience is to change the way you perceive that experience. The same event can be perceived as barely tolerable or highly enjoyable, depending on how you choose to think about it. For instance, the breakup of a marriage could be a *terrible tragedy* or it could be a *terrific threshold* for a new and greater love to come into your life. Your interpretation of an experience determines its outcome in your life even down to your facial expressions. Whether you react to something with a frown or smile is up to you, but what would you rather do?

Ask yourself, *Am I enduring my life or enjoying my life?*

Circumstances happen the way that they do as a result of your thoughts about those circumstances. People are buffeted around by circumstances as long as they allow themselves to be affected by outside conditions and don't realize that they are in control. In reality, you can only control one person, and that person is *you*. It is much easier to change what you are doing (which is in your control) than to try to change what someone else is doing. Until you can say, *I chose that. It was my fault*, you can't change anything.

Once you make up your mind that you are in control, your mind begins creating your life. There are actually two kinds of control.

Internal control

This means that you are in control of your own life. As a result, anything bad that happens in your life is your fault. By the same token, anything good that happens, you deserve credit for. You do not choose all the events and circumstances in your life; but you do control your reactions to and interpretations of those events, which produce either happy or sad emotions about that event. Remember, an event is just an event and is emotionally neutral. It's your perception of an event that makes it personal to you and triggers a smile or a frown. Choosing to *act or react* has been programmed in you from the inside.

When you operate under internal control, the choice is yours to face the future with either *apprehension* or *anticipation*. You decide which choice will produce the better results. Take the challenge. Get excited! Don't just face each day, *embrace* each day! When you are fully in touch with your heart's desire and can clearly visualize what it is that you want, the universe will show you how to get it. Once you utilize the creative power within you and seize control of your own life, your life will become what you want it to be. Begin living by design and design a happy life for yourself.

External control

This means you are allowing someone else to control your life because you are letting someone else or something else make your decisions for you. This also means that whatever bad that happens in your life, *you* take no responsibility for having created. Likewise, then, you can take no credit for whatever good that happens in your life. External control is like choosing to go through life as a marionette with strings attached to each part of your body. Then you give one string to your spouse, one to your parents, one to your children, and one to your boss. When you go through life with the mental mindset that says to the world, *"Pull my string, and I'll do anything"*, you are under external control. When you do not make your own choices or determine your own happiness, you are not in control of your own life. No wonder you feel empty and hollow inside! When you have a wooden head, you certainly cannot create or carry out your own wishes. Giuseppe needs to breathe life into you, making you a real live person, because giving the control of your life to others is no life at all! It would be much better to be a real-life Pinocchio than to be a marionette! When you do take control of your own life,—yes, you will make mistakes, learn lessons, and possibly be led astray when you make bad decisions; but at least, you will be living your own life and doing what you want without the *disease to please*.

When you feel that you are ready to take control of your own life, ask yourself, *"what would an ideal life look like to me? How can I make my mental pictures into my reality?"*

We all came to this planet for a purpose. Listen to life. You're the only one who can hear your own heart strings and the tune they're playing. *Be You-nique!* Learn to think for yourself. Life will show you what to do and how to do it once you have defined your desires. Tell life what you want out of it, and let the universe take care of the details. Find your core self that loves life and see what an ideal life looks like to you.

Move toward the moments of joy within you. Listen to the longing for life inside of you. You can't get this same feeling from the outside— from external places or people. Real feelings and beliefs have to come from inside of you. *If there isn't a temple in your heart, you won't find your heart in a temple!* Just going to church won't make you a Christian any more than sleeping in the garage will make you a Cadillac! The feelings, beliefs, and desires have to come from inside of you.

Be the driver in your own life, not a passenger! Your physical body can be the car; but let your soul be the driver, and your spirit be the gas. Decide where you want to go, and then drive yourself there. Let your feelings be your compass, and your desires be the ignition switch. Now, turn life on!

Wherever you are right now is exactly where you need to be. When you are ready to move on, you will—once you get that you are in control and have the power to change. Focus on the *positive* of what you want out of life. You can't get rich by just hating poverty. Think instead of having abundance in your life. Picture what abundance looks like to you—whether it is an abundance of riches, love, or health, that you want. (Remember there is wealth in wellness, too!) Focus on what you love and draw that to you.

If you want to change your external circumstances, go within. *Go within and you'll never do without!* Most people think that they have to go out and create wealth and possessions first in order to determine who they are, but it is more important to discover who you are first, and then to go out and create what you want.

Unless you change how you think, you will always have what you have right now. That is what your current thinking has created for you. If you're happy with your life and what you have, that is wonderful. If not, it is up to *you* to do something to change your life. To keep doing the same thing every day and to expect the outcome to be any different is ludicrous.

That kind of thinking reminds me of a bird who appears at my window every spring. In an attempt to get in, the bird rams his head against my window, which makes a loud noise and must stun the bird.

For some reason, the bird just keeps trying again and again to get in the closed window, even though the outcome is always the same. Every time the bird hits his head, he must experience pain; but he won't give up. After about twenty unsuccessful attempts, the bird finally flies away; but he'll be back the next day to try again. How foolish of the bird to expect the outcome to be any different when he keeps doing the same thing over and over. Why doesn't the bird just look for an open window or fly to where his destination is unobstructed? The bird just doesn't think of that—I guess that's because he has a *bird brain*!

It must be very painful for God, in his wisdom, to watch us, as human beings, ram our heads every day in the same way. Under his breath, God must mutter,

When will they ever learn?

4

Determining the Future

Time is priceless, yet it costs us nothing! You can do anything you want with your time, but you can't own it. Time is like having a bucket of water and trying to take the water out of the bucket with your hand. You can drink from the bucket and enjoy the water, but you can't grasp the water or try to hold on to it.

You can spend time or throw it away, but you can't keep it. Once you've lost it, there's no getting it back. The only thing you have control over is *how* you spend your time. You can spend your time in any way you want—that is in happiness, peace, and love; or you can spend your time in anger, resentment, bitterness, and boredom. Whatever commodity you get in exchange for your time is up to you, but you must spend it. The best thing you can do is to spend your time wisely and get something worthwhile in return for it—like a happy memory. Don't trade your time too cheaply. After all, what is worth more than this day?

Time flies on its own! Our role is simply to be the pilot or navigator and determine where it goes. What are you doing with your time? Where are you directing it to go? Are you creating happy memories in exchange for your time by living the life that you want? If not, why not?

Often there is just a fine line between the life we have and the life we really want. Why can't we just cross over that line or use an eraser to erase it?

Since *life is not a dress rehearsal*, we don't get to do it over again. We don't even get to choose how and when we die, but we do get to choose how and where we live. Just make sure that when you do die, you *die alive* because you have been living every moment of your life. Don't just *roll over and play dead* before you die!

In the middle of the word *LIVE* are the letters *i* and *v*. Some of us need to use that **I.V.** and get injected **I**nter**V**eineously in order to really be al-**IV**-e. When are you going to start to l-**IV**-e? Ask yourself, "*What am I waiting for? What needs to happen before I can do what I have been postponing? What do I need to have before I can do what I want? From whom am I waiting to get permission?*"

It's never too late to live happily ever after! Fairytales do come true—but only the ones that you create yourself. Today's dreams determine tomorrow's reality. Yesterday determined *what was*. Today determines *what could be* and influences the future into *what will be*.

Your future can actually be determined in one of *three* ways:

1– By Crisis.

Are you a *master of disaster?* Many people live their lives going from crisis to crisis (which they actually create in their lives to avoid having to make any positive plans!) It's almost as if these people couldn't be happy unless there was something climatic and chaotic happening in their lives at all times.

How many times have you heard someone say, "*If I didn't have bad luck, I wouldn't have any luck at all?*" What do you think that person is creating in their life? Some people dwell on negative thoughts and events because they believe that's all they deserve in life. Subsequently, they generate the results that they believe they deserve. It's almost as if these people have a dark cloud over their heads at all times, causing it to rain only on them. Make no mistake about who is pulling the string to get that cloud to follow them. If these people would let go of the string, the cloud would float away; and the sun would shine again. A person doesn't really have to see the sun to know that it's there, but you can't see a sunset or a rainbow by looking down!

How many people continually blame others for what happens to them without ever realizing that they are in control and that they are creating whatever is happening in their own lives? Many people actually choose to be victims by complaining about what others are doing *to* them. When you allow yourself to become *victimized*, you become *paralyzed*. On the other hand, if you live your life with *purpose*, you are in harmony with your source; and a crisis will not cripple you. The worst thing that you could ever conceive of happening to you might be the best thing that could ever happen to you when you don't let things get the best of you.

It is actually through crisis that one creates—by either creating chaos or cheer. The choice is really up to you. Remember, *today is the tomorrow you worried about yesterday.* Since our tomorrows are created by today's thoughts, why not create *You-phoria?*

2– By Chance.

Good things can come into your life by chance. You could hit the lottery, inherit a fortune, or make it big on *American Idol*. Negative things can also happen by chance—the loss of a loved one, a debilitating illness, or a crash in the stock market. Chance is something you have no control over that brings good events or bad events into your life. You can only control your reaction to whatever chance may bring.

Some people refer to chance as *LUCK*. In the middle of the word *LUCK* are the letters *u* and *c*, which stand for U Create, so you see that what you call luck is really what you create. How do you create? You create by your reactions. Your reactions are your choice. For instance, you can decide whether to curse the rain for ruining your picnic or your wedding or to regard rain as a blessing or good luck for the farmer who is desperately trying to water his crop. When you curse

45

the rain, you negate any good that it does. Instead, learn to appreciate the rain. Where would we be without it? Look for the blessings in any situation. The interpretation of any event is up to you, but you will act in accordance with the way you perceive that event. *Learn to dance in the rain*! Remember, opportunities often come disguised as misfortunes! Many times, we just don't recognize our blessings because they come dressed in pain, fear, or tears.

3– By Choice.

Choice is the key to creating your life. Once you understand that you have a choice and exercise your ability to make a choice, you create powerfully with each choice that you make. Since you are responsible for your choices, you must be willing to accept the consequences of those choices. However, you must choose. The person who does not make a choice actually *chooses* not to make a choice. Sometimes your choices are between something bad and something worse; but, thank God, you still have the choice! Don't confuse a tough choice with no choice at all. It is better to have a choice, no matter how difficult that choice may be. Prisoners have no choice. Slaves had no choice. Thank God you have a choice and a voice! Wouldn't you rather have a choice than to have your choices made for you by someone else?

Your future can be determined by *crisis, chance, or choice*. Which method of determining your future would you choose? Remember, your choice creates the consequences.

When you are about to make a choice about something, *Play it Forward*. Before you make any important choice, ask yourself two questions:

1. What results will this choice produce?
2. Am I willing to accept the consequences of this choice?

Each choice creates its own set of consequences that you will have to live with. If you make the wrong choice, you will have to suffer the consequences. But until you can say, *I chose that. It was my fault*, you can't change anything. When you take responsibility for your choices and your actions, you are taking control of your life. Thank God we have the chance to make a choice, which also implies that we can make a choice to change.

Make wise choices by weighing the consequences of each choice before making that choice. Don't emotionally or impulsively rush into any choice, but be grateful that you have the choice. If someone else were making all your choices in life for you, that person would own you— and slavery has been abolished! When you are following someone else's rules, you are not thinking, leading, or growing. You are obeying. Cut the strings and chose for yourself.

It is not just what happens to us in life that matters; it is what we choose to do about what happens to us that makes the difference in how our lives turn out. Success is getting what you want. Happiness is wanting what you get. Make a contract with yourself to stay focused on the positive and learn to *discipline your disappointments.* If you allow yourself to be disappointed by what others do, then others control you. Your choice is to be happy, regardless of what others do. Your happiness should depend on only one person, and that person is you! Happiness is not an accident or something you just wish for. It's something you design and let flow from within. Happiness and hatred are both boomerangs. Whatever you throw out comes right back to you. Don't hoard happiness. Give it away. It will come back to you and bring all its friends with it!

A positive attitude is an inside job! Would you get an A on your attitude or do you have a Baditude? Attitudes are contagious. Is yours worth catching? Just as we nurture our bodies with the right nutrients and vitamin supplements, we need to nurture our minds with good thoughts. We also need to exercise our minds by creating those thoughts into reality.

Attitude is actually much more important in life than *aptitude,* but look at the time we spend getting an education, thinking that a degree is going to change our lives! If our lives aren't working, we have to first look at making internal changes and *attitude adjustments.*

Change can be brought into our lives in one of two ways—either through *inspiration* or *desperation*. Wouldn't it be better if we were *inspired* to change as good positive energy flowed through us setting up a spark that lit our light bulb? Inspiration is like electricity. We don't have to understand electricity to know that it exists. We just have to believe that it exists and flick on the switch. People don't walk into a room and look for the *dark switch*. They turn on the *light*! Switch on your spiritual electricity (your inspiration) by accessing your higher source of power and let it illuminate your path. Once you are *enlightened*, use your electricity as enthusiasm to light up others. Watch that positive energy flow just as in a row of light bulbs where one after another light bulb is magically turned on. When energy flows in a row, it is exciting to watch because of its power to overcome the dark.

If you are trying to flick on your mental switch and find that you are still in the dark, check to see if your eyes are open. Don't act out of desperation. Scary creatures live only in the dark. Open your eyes, and they will go away. Monsters are not real anyway—just a fabrication of your fears. Remember things that upset you can also inspire you. Dwell on the upbeat. Think from the end. See yourself surrounded by the conditions you want to create in your life by acting like they are already here. *Get away from woulda, coulda, shouda,* and implement *do, did, and done!*

You create your life continuously by the choices that you make. Each morning when you wake up, say to yourself, *Today, I can choose to be in a good mood or a bad mood. I choose to be in a good mood.* If something unpleasant happens that day, you can choose to dwell on it and become a victim of that circumstance, or you can look for the lesson and move on. Instead of asking, *Why me?* ask *What can I learn from this event?*

When someone else comes to you complaining, you can choose to compound their complaints, thereby wallowing in the muck with them; or you can point out the positive side of life. If you don't stay positive, and choose instead to join in their negativity, it is possible to promulgate a *chain of pain*; but you can't feel bad enough for anyone else to feel better. Wouldn't it be better to help that other person feel good because you feel good? Program only positives into your life. Make yourself feel good by only concentrating on what you want, not on what you don't want or what another person is feeling bad about.

Remember, you *receive what you request*. Thoughts are mental requests. Just make sure they are positive because you get out what you are putting in. Imagine sitting down in front of your computer and asking it *not* to give you information about a certain subject. Try this. I did! If you go to Google and ask it specifically to *not* give you information about a bichon frise, the computer will give you information on this breed of dog anyway. Wow! Your mind actually works the same way. Although your mind is so much more powerful than a computer, it cannot interpret your thoughts. Your mind focuses on any picture you give it. Your mind hears the words you input and the pictures you imprint, but it does not hear the *not!* Your subconscious cannot understand why you would be thinking about or picturing something that you do not want any more than a computer can understand why you would be asking for information that you do not want. Your mind, like a computer, will access the subject matter you are giving it. Since your thoughts have the power to manifest anything you ardently desire, why focus on something you ardently do *not* desire when the results you get are directly based on the recipe. *All things are actually created twice—first in your own mind, then in real life!*

Focus on *I want to feel good*, and act that out all day. In fact, in my *feel-good-place* down the ocean, our voice message actually says:

"Hello, this is Rick and Elaine's happy hideaway, and we want to feel good. If the purpose of your message is to do anything other than that, please call Dr. Phil!"

Try to think only positive thoughts because negative thoughts will weigh you down and smother you. The heaviest thing you can carry in life is a grudge. Holding a grudge against someone or something is like letting sludge live inside of you. If you let the little green Mucinex man move into your heart, he'll take over and will smother all your happiness until you can't breathe. Kick the sucker out so joy and happiness can move in. If something is upsetting you, address it and deal with it immediately. Otherwise, the fungus will fester.

Your happiness can be tempered by your interpretation of external events, which may or may not meet your expectations; but remember who created those expectations. For instance, if you were taking a vacation in the Caribbean and expected warm, sunny beach weather every day but found that each day was less than 60 degrees, you would indeed be disappointed. However, if you were visiting Canada or Alaska (especially in the winter), a day just under 60 degrees would seem like a very warm, pleasant day. Clearly, happiness and disappointment then are the direct result of your expectations. Your expectations actually determine your experience of reality. Sometimes, it is easier to change your expectations than it is to change reality. No event is actually good or bad on its own until it is given a label in your mind.

Learn to read between the minds!

In the middle of life there is always an "*if*." The "*if*" is the "**I**-**F**actor." When you get that you are in control of your life, the "*if*" will be taken out of it. Begin to create the life that you want. Take the "*if*" out of life. Instead, give yourself an *i.v.* and live!

Leave yesterday behind—along with any of its problems, worries, and doubts. The past has passed. Turn your wounds into wisdom by learning from each lesson, then move on! Clear your mind by pulling it out of the past so that instead you can focus on a fantastic future. Once you make new, clear choices, your life can be anything you want it to be!

All we really have is the *now*, but now reversed is *won*. *Seize the now, reverse it, and you will continually be a winner.*

Life is *what it is*, but it can become *what you make it*! We are all a *work in progress*!

Dreams are the directives that put our priorities in place!

5

Self-Image

The three most powerful words in the English language are:

I am ....

and whatever word you choose to end that sentence with. Your perception of who you are actually preempts the reality of who you become. *Who you see is who you'll be!* Until you can discover who you really are, you are projecting who you aren't.

WHO ARE YOU?

Your self-image is what you believe to be true about yourself. You will act in accordance with the image and the mental picture you have in your mind of who you really are. The reason it's called a *self-image* is that it's an opinion *of* yourself, *by* yourself, and *for* yourself! Yet, if you think of *self* as a four-letter dirty word (meaning that you think it is wrong to be selfish), you will proceed to give yourself away. However, the truth is that until you can truly value yourself and know who you are, you have nothing to give away.

Don't accept anyone else's definition of your true self. Learn to define yourself by yourself. Why is it that most people are lost when it comes to defining who they really are? If you can't seem to define yourself, you might ask yourself, *Where did I lose me?*

When you think highly of yourself and project that lofty image, the world will take you at your own estimate. Why is it, though, that most of us would rather rely on other people's opinions about who we are? Most people would rather accept another person's opinion as reality than to define for themselves who they really are. That would be like a young girl wandering into a fun house to find out who she really was. Standing in front of one distorted mirror, the young girl may see herself as short and fat. Saying to herself *"Surely, that's not me"*, the girl hears an echo of voices from family and friends saying, "Oh yes, that's you. That looks just like you!" Unwilling to accept this opinion of herself, the girl moves on to another mirror, where she becomes long and lean. Although the young girl knows inside that this image is really not her either, she hears another echo of voices that say, *"That's you. That looks exactly like you!"* Some people might just stop there and accept the voices and other people's opinions about who they really are, while others would move on to yet a third mirror. *Don't listen to those voices outside of you.* Keep moving from mirror to mirror until what you see in the mirror is the person you want to be—one that reflects who you truly are. Then step into that mirror and become that person permanently. The self you want to see doesn't have to be reflected in somebody else's eyes. Project the prettiest part of you from the inside until that is what everyone else sees on the outside. Next time you look in your mirror, ask yourself, *"when will my reflection show the real me—who I truly am inside?"*

A mirror is objective. It reflects back anything that is put in front of it. However, what you choose to see in the mirror is subjective. Do you see the beautiful person you are on the inside, or do you see all the lines and wrinkles that are forming on the outside? Do you see a serene soul or a sagging body? Do you see just the wrapping of the package or the treasure that lies inside? Do you tell yourself that you love the inside of the person in the mirror, or are you only concerned with the outside frame? The mirror can only reflect what you choose to see. Once you realize that every line on your face is the result of too much laughter and every wrinkle marks the spot where a smile has been, you will be grateful for those lines and wrinkles. Your self-image is really a *self-portrait*. What are you choosing to see and paint about yourself? Actually, you are repainting your portrait everyday. Don't make your portrait a *tale of two selves*. Decide on the best you, and let your inner glow show!

Live up to your own potential. No one hears your inner voice and your inner calling of inspiration except you. When you listen to your own inner voice, you will not fall into frustration. Conceive thoughts of what the best you could look like. Once you conceive higher thoughts of who you could be, those thoughts will, like a cocoon, wrap silken threads of grander visions around you until the beautiful butterfly that is really you emerges. No longer will you be a creepy crawly caterpillar that other people can step on.

Be your own best friend by asking yourself, "*Who would I be and what would I do if I didn't have to worry about the opinions of others?*" Then ask yourself, "*What price am I paying for trying to please others? Is it worth it?*" Are you a public success and a private failure? Or is your own jury still out about you?

Become independent of the good opinion of others! The people who get the most approval in life are the people who don't care about anyone's approval but their own. Don't let others decide who you are. You are the only one who can correctly determine that. Decide for yourself that your life is powerful. Your life is worthy. When you're going in the right direction, all resistance will turn into respect as you grow into greatness! If you don't believe you can do great things right away, then try doing small things, but in a great way! The difference between *ordinary* and *extraordinary* is just that little *extra!*

If the person you see in the mirror is not who you would really like to be, change your self-image. Start by being aware of more than what you wear. If you don't follow your inner flair, you'll get nowhere. Your self-image is determined not only by who you are now, but who you really want to be—that person that you visualize yourself as being. You can change your self-image by changing your thoughts about yourself. Don't be envious of anyone else, or you block out the real beauty that is you.

Wear your self-image like a suit of armor whose purpose is to protect you. No arrows from others can get in to pierce your ego once you truly know who you are. When you are secure in the who of who you really are, other people's opinions won't really matter. Tell yourself, *"I am in a state of pre-magnificence, but I am on a magnificent mission."* Then try being the most magnificent version of the greatest vision you can have of yourself. Just like Don Quixote in *Man of La Mancha*, proceed with your vision without worrying about the world mocking you. Opinions of others don't really matter as long as your vision is stronger than their short-sightedness.

Don't be a *mini-me*. Be a *mega-me* by being all that you can be! Like the tin man in the *Wizard of Oz*, once you find your heart, lead with it. When your heart is truly strong enough, no one can trump it. History is full of many battles and contests that have been won by heart alone.

When people hurl insults at you, laugh at them. Coat your self with Teflon so insults won't stick. Humor desensitizes insults so they cannot sting you, and actually makes them roll off you like water off a duck's back. When you can make jokes in response to other people's insults, it just shows how secure you are inside. Know that *mediocrity always attacks magnificence.* When someone calls me a *bitch* (and don't think they haven't!), I actually thank them because my definition of a *bitch* is a <u>B</u>abe <u>I</u>n <u>T</u>otal <u>C</u>ontrol of <u>H</u>erself. When I respond with a thank you to this insult and share my definition of a bitch, I take away any power from the other person's put-down by deeming it a compliment. Their anger actually turns into laughter and then respect. When you can laugh at insults instead of getting offended, usually others will laugh with you. People actually like to be around a person who has so totally accepted herself that she can laugh at insults and not be offended by them. You cannot insult a person who will not let herself be insulted because she is so secure about who she is. The insult then has no effect whatsoever, except to reflect badly on whoever originated it.

Another visualization I find very helpful, especially for the ladies, is to visualize yourself as a good witch floating in a bubble, giving out love to everyone around you. Light and love flow out of the bubble to everyone you come in contact with, but the bubble (which is plastic on the outside) lets in no insults or negative thoughts. The insults bounce off the bubble and right back at whoever is sending them. Since thoughts are boomerangs, whatever someone is thinking or putting out goes right back to the original sender. On the other hand, you could choose to be a bad witch. A bad witch is one who hurls negative thoughts and curses toward others. She is certainly not welcomed anywhere or even pleasant to be around. The choice is up to you! Which witch do you want to be?

When a woman finally gets in touch with her inner *BITCH*, no one will ever belittle her again! Try to make yourself into the kind of woman about whom, when your feet hit the floor each morning, the devil says, *"Oh no! She's up!"*

Rebuild yourself from the inside out with a strong sense of self that radiates confidence and demands respect from the moment you walk into a room. When you walk into a room like you own it, people will flock to be around you. They really want to try to understand your own good opinion of you. If you can maintain that lofty opinion of yourself; pretty soon, others will begin to agree with you.

There is a perfume on the market which illustrates this point. The perfume is called *Realm* and is supposedly made from pheromones. Pheromones are natural hormonal secretions of the body, which are supposed to attract the opposite sex. I believe that the pheromones in this perfume were taken from butterflies, but the perfume is advertised as a powerful sexual magnet that works on humans to attract the opposite sex. The purpose of this perfume (when worn by a woman) is to attract any male—making that male feel sexually aroused just by sniffing her (at least that's what the ad said!). Many women have said that it works, too! Actually, I maintain that it isn't really the perfume, but a woman's *belief* about the perfume that works when that woman is wearing it. When a woman walks into a room, chest out, wearing pheromones, and actually believes that any male who smells her will instantly be attracted to her, guess what? The question then becomes, *is it really the pheromones, or the belief that a woman has about herself when she is wearing pheromones that make the perfume work?* Anyone with a *belief* about herself that she is irresistibly loveable becomes automatically lovable, and you can actually save the money for the perfume!

Actually, if you love you, everyone else will too. Bathe yourself in the belief that you are beautiful, and just see what happens. When the time comes in your life, that *to remain tight in the bud becomes more painful than to burst into bloom*, you will blossom into the beautiful flower you were meant to be. After all, if nothing ever changed, there would be no butterflies. Let your inner butterfly out! Don't stay shut up in your cocoon. Remember that just when the caterpillar thought it was all over, it became a butterfly! If that happens in nature every day, why not in human nature too?

Staying in touch with your inner core or soul builds up your self-esteem from within. Don't just love yourself on the outside; love all of you—inside and out. Real beauty lies on the inside—the side of you that you seldom show! Let your real beauty out, and people won't care what you look like on the outside. Actually, we pick our friends from the inside out. We don't pick our friends for what they look like on the outside. If we did, then the prettiest people would have the most friends; but that is seldom the case. We pick our real friends for who they are on the inside, once we get to know them. We pick our friends for their hearts. I say that one of my best friends is *all heart*, because that is what I see when I look at her. When you get in touch with your own inner beauty, you will discover who you are at heart and unlock your real power. The power is within you to be anything you want to be, once you get in touch with that power.

There is a little story I like to use to illustrate this point. It's from a third grade reading book.

There once was a spirit named Hofus, who lived in a rock, where he was very unassuming and oblivious to the world around him. One day, Hofus heard a *tap, tap, tap* and looked up to see a rock cutter chipping away at him. All of a sudden, Hofus realized that he had no control over his life because there was something out there that was more powerful than he was. That thought was very disturbing to Hofus, so he began wishing and praying to the powers that be, *If Hofus only a rock cutter could be!*

The powers that be turned Hofus into a rock cutter. He was very content with his new life until, one day, he noticed a king driving by in a golden carriage. Realizing that the king was richer and more powerful than he was, Hofus became envious and started to chant, *"Ah me, if Hofus only a king could be!"*

Once again, Hofus was transformed by the powers that be, and this time into a king. Hofus was happy for a long time being a king, until he finally realized there was something even more powerful than a king. When Hofus looked up at the sky, he noticed the sun, which seemed to be the center of life because it could control when people got up in the morning and went to bed at night, could cause things to grow, or could scorch the earth. Hofus was sure that the sun was the most powerful thing in the universe. Hofus chanted, *"Ah me, if Hofus only the sun could be!"*

The powers that be changed Hofus into the sun. He was sure that he now was the most powerful thing on Earth—until one day, a cloud came by. Hofus noticed that, as the sun, he could not control the cloud, which got in the way of his rays, creating cloudy days and rain. As hard as Hofus would shine, he had no effect on the Earth once a cloud got in the way. Hofus no longer felt all-powerful, and said to himself, *"Ah me, if Hofus only a cloud could be."*

The powers that be turned Hofus into a cloud, and he now had fun raining on people's picnics and causing crops to grow or to wither. People would pray for him to either come or go away. However, there was still one thing that Hofus noticed that he had no effect over whatsoever. It was a rock! As the sun, Hofus noticed that as hard as he would shine on the rock, he could not affect it with his heat. Also, as a cloud, Hofus could not affect the rock with rain. Slowly, Hofus began to realize once again that there was something even more powerful than he was, and started chanting, *"Ah me, if Hofus only a rock could be!"*

The powers that be turned Hofus into a rock, which, as you know, was exactly where he had started. There was a big difference now, though! Hofus had discovered that he was the most powerful force in the universe, because the power was in him to be anything or to do anything he wanted. Hofus was still the same form on the outside, but different somehow inside. Now he knew how powerful he was—so powerful that he could create for himself the most coveted thing in the world—peace and contentment! Hofus never thought of himself as a lowly rock again. He was a *supreme being* in the shape of a rock!

Isn't that what we all are? Supreme beings inhabiting whatever earthly forms we choose on the outside. When you really believe that you are the most powerful being in the world on the inside, you won't let anything or anyone stop you from being whatever you want to be on the outside.

The power to be anything you want to be is within you. It starts with a wish or a desire, and then blossoms into a belief that you must empower with passion. That power is priceless, but you must protect your power. Be particular about whom you share it with. Don't just give your power away. When you relate to another person, ask yourself, *Does this person empower me or drain me, appreciate me or annoy me?* Knowing that you have a choice, why would you choose to be around people who drain or annoy you?

The opposite of being in touch with your power and being in control of your own life is choosing to be a victim. By allowing yourself to become a victim, you are actually giving your power away and putting someone else in control of your life. You become a victim by blaming others for things that happen to you over which you claim to have no control. In reality, you can only be a victim once. After that you're a volunteer! Drop your victim story. (We all have one, you know!) Victims look for empathy as a method of exerting control over others; but *victimization* is really *paralyzation* since you cannot act if you have no control over your own actions.

Some people choose to paralyze their future by constantly reliving their past. These people fail to realize that they are not their past, which they can't seem to *get past*. The past has passed! However, many people still prefer to live in the past (perhaps it's because it's cheaper there!). You are not your past, and you can't go back and change it. All you can do is learn from it. Consider the possibility of who you could be in the future once you take control of your life and realize your own power. If someone has wronged you in the past, forgive that person. That wrong happened to create whatever lesson you needed to learn from it. Thank that person for the lesson, and move on. Forgiveness is actually just giving up the belief that the past could have been any different.

Forgiveness is also the realization that no single person or event can take away your happiness *forever!* You can't fight for a better past, but you can create a better future by letting go of the past. *Get past your past!* Forgive people who have hurt you in the past for your sake, not theirs, and take your power back. Decide that no one will be in charge of your life again except you, and that you will never be a victim again. That means that you have to take responsibility for your own life and cannot blame anyone or anything else for your actions—not even the devil!

To say *"The devil made me do it"* is an attempt to absolve yourself from taking any responsibility for your own behavior. I gave up the belief in a devil about the same time that I gave up a belief in Santa Claus and the Easter Bunny (who at least had good intentions and love as their basis). I cannot believe that mature adults really do believe in Satan or the devil, yet I hear him referenced a lot. To believe in a little man dressed up in a red suit with horns on his head and a pitchfork in his hand is ludicrous. Trying to visualize the devil jumping up and down in glee while someone's soul is burning for eternity is even more ridiculous. First of all, souls have no body to burn! So what burns, if the soul is eternal? To blame something that you did (which obviously you were not proud of or you would have taken credit for) on a mythical creature is just escaping from reality and looking for a scapegoat on which to blame your actions. The devil is you! If you did something wrong, acknowledge it, and take responsibility for the consequences. Don't blame evil on external influences. Evil is only you moving away from your source. If you accidently made a wrong turn onto that *exit marked Evil*, do a quick U-turn back to your source, which creates all the good in your life. That is the only way you will be able to change your behavior in the future.

Evil cannot create. It can only destroy. When you say, *"The devil made me do it"*, you are admitting that you had no control over your own behavior. Since you obviously have no control over the devil (even if one did exist), you therefore cannot change your behavior. The devil could keep making you exhibit bad behavior, time after time, since supposedly that's what a devil does! That thought is ludicrous and totally wrong! Why give control to anything outside of you when, in reality, you are just giving your own power away? I can't believe that anyone would consciously want to do that! When someone invokes the concept of a devil, that person is really just looking for someone else to blame his own bad behavior on. Most people have trouble acknowledging that their own behavior (which they are obviously ashamed of) was motivated by their own envy or evil desires. If you cannot accept the blame for your bad behavior, you cannot take credit for your good behavior. When you say *"It was not my fault"* when it was, it means you are not willing to take responsibility for your own actions. Until you can step up to the plate and say *"Mea culpa* (it was my fault)"*, you can't change anything! You see, you can't really change something until you acknowledge the responsibility for having created it in the first place. When you take responsibility for your own behavior, at least you are admitting that you are in control of your own life. You have to own your behavior before you can disown it!

To be in control means owning up to the good and bad that you do—not giving anyone else the credit or blame for it. Stay in control of your own life by not entertaining evil thoughts or emotions about anyone else. Act only out of love or kind thoughts, and the devil in you will disappear. Evil cannot emanate from someone who feels only joy and love within. *Evil cannot abide where love resides!*

Never attempt to retaliate if someone has hurt you or excluded you on purpose by mimicking their poor behavior. Then they are, in effect, controlling you and changing you. To be better than they are, ignore the slight and simply walk away. Choose happiness over the lesser gods of revenge or righteousness.

Notice a pattern in the people you attract. The people you draw to you are your mirrors and reflect what you are putting out. Do you like the reflection of yourself that you see in their eyes? If you attract people who don't respect you, it's because you don't respect yourself. Are you getting love and respect from your mirrors? If people constantly mistreat you, take a closer look at the image that you are projecting to them. You draw to you what you give out. Give out kindness—you get kindness back. Give out love—you get love back.

Now imagine attracting only the kind of people you would like to have in your life, who love and respect you because you love and respect yourself. One of the nicest compliments I received recently was from a classmate of mine from college. She said that I had been blessed with both beauty and brains, but that I had chosen to use my brains rather than my beauty, which was very unusual. This certainly made me feel good and made me want to be around that person even more. People do not mirror your outside, they mirror your inside. Are your insides worth mirroring? If not, it's up to you to change your image until you like what you see in the mirror. Polish your mirror until it reflects the true you.

Take a look at your life. The next time you interact with a person, stop and ask yourself, *Does this person give me energy by motivating me, inspiring me, or providing comfort, love, and support? Or is this person sapping my energy with their negative comments and emotions?* In a true friendship, there should be a balance of giving and receiving good energy from both parties.

Sometimes, someone's ego gets in the way. E.G.O. stands for *Edging God Out*. Instead of just letting the love that's in their hearts shine forth, most people worry more about what they look like on the outside because they think that others are judging them on that basis alone. Unless and until you know who you are on the inside, you are vulnerable to other people's opinions.

How many people do you know who do everything they can to look like *Vogue* on the outside, but are vague inside? External appearances have become so important that some people, women in particular, will spend a fortune on botox, cosmetic surgery, liposuction, veneers, hair products, and makeup to look good on the outside. Many women think they could be a *man-magnet* if they looked good enough on the outside. I think that these women are underestimating men—at least most of them! Wouldn't it be better if those women spent the same time and money developing a magnetic personality? Looks might attract someone from across a room and make that person want to meet you; but it takes a much stronger magnet, like intelligence, humor, confidence, and caring, to keep that person by your side. Work on your inside first. A man might fall *in lust* with a beautiful body, but he falls in love with what's on the inside—the real you. Rather than trying to look like a model, be a good role model for the world to see! Not only will you like yourself better, but the world will too!

Build your treasures on the inside and invest in the inner you. After all, we are not our bodies, which, despite all our efforts, will only grow old. We are really the spirit who is inhabiting our body for a short time. Just like when you go on a cruise, you may reside in a cabin or a suite for a week or a month; but you are not that cabin or suite. That is just your temporary quarters, however expanded or cramped they might be. You are the spirit that resides inside that cabin. Make sure your spirit shines!

Your physical body is just the housing or frame that holds your soul. Think of your body as a television. There is the outside casing, but that is not what produces the picture. It simply holds the picture. If it were not for the electricity or energy inside, there would be no picture. Our souls are the electricity —an energy that turns the set on and creates the picture. Our thoughts are the remote control. We can control what we see by changing the channel until we get a picture and a story about our life that is pleasing to us. Ultimately, we are in control, not of the energy, which is always there (whether we turn the set on or not), but of the story or program that unfolds, once we tune in to the right channel. By controlling our thoughts, we can control the story of our life. Some of us may tune in to HDTV, some of us get regular TV. It's up to each individual to decide what picture he or she wants to create about his or her life. There are programs out there that we haven't even heard of yet. Be open to them!

If you choose to play the same story over and over, you will live the same circumstances over and over. The places and the faces may be different; but if the story is always the same, *your life is a rerun!* Tell a different story. Tell the story of your life the way you want it to be. After all, it is your story and your life. You are the creator of your own life experience, whether you want to be the creator or not. *True life* only means someone thought it into being. Everything starts as a thought first before it takes physical form since we are source energy in physical bodies.

Your life is what you say it is. True power occurs when your personality aligns with your soul's goals. Authentic power can never be taken away from you if it comes from the core of your soul, where love and peace reside. Then what others think of you doesn't really matter. The only person whose opinion really matters is your own. It's what *you* think of *you* that creates *you* each and every day. Don't miss out on being *you* by playing a role that isn't *you*! Begin to tell the story of your life as you want it to be, not as what it has been, if what it has been has not been happy. If you really want to change *what is*, conceive of *what is not* as something you would really like to have in your life. Then act as if *what is not* were *now here*, as you believe it into being. Embrace that essential essence of excitement that you have created and capture it before it eludes you. You know what you want in life and what you do not want. Focus on only what you want, and it will fabricate.

Don't be like an oyster, which is an ugly, scaly thing on the outside, but is soft and vulnerable on the inside. That's where the good stuff is. However, an oyster has to be dead before anyone can enjoy the good stuff. Don't let that happen to you. Allow yourself to be vulnerable. When you let others into your shell, sometimes they may irritate you; but you can turn that irritation into a pearl. Life should not be lived shut down inside a shell. Let people get to know the real you by opening up. You will be surprised at the treasures that will come in, and what pearls you will be able to produce.

Sometimes, when the world is irritating you and you are feeling stressed, check your thinking. Ask yourself, *What am I feeling so stressed about?* Turn that stress into strength. Sometimes, when the world is too much with me, and I feel like I am losing my essence, that's when I have to stop and get in touch with my *inner elf*. At times, when I get overwhelmed and bogged down with too much to do, I just have to stop and let the *fairies* take over. Diane, a very wise woman, once suggested this to me; and I said, *"Fairies? Hey, you're right. I need some fairies in my life! Where can I buy fairies or rent them?"* Then, suddenly I realized that you can't buy or rent fairies. You can only *believe* in them, and they will come. Sometimes, my fairies are personified by my husband, a family member, a friend, or even a stranger; but they are always there to help when I need them. *It's up to me to believe;* and, sometimes, I just have to back off and let *the fairies take over!*

If you don't deal with stress, it will turn into frustration and anger. Anger is a strong emotion (strong enough to get your attention!) Anger is telling you that you are losing power to external circumstances. Frustration and resentment are anger's first cousins. They are all part of the *Feeling Family* and guess who is the head of that family? Yes, you have a right to be angry; but you have a right to be happy, too. Which is the better choice for you to make? Remember, one minute spent in anger is sixty seconds of happiness lost. All you really have to lose is your life—minute by minute. Don't lose control to negative emotions, because then you are allowing those emotions to take over. When you're feeling angry, what you're really feeling is fear or frustration that you are not in control. When you indulge your anger by telling someone off or putting them down, you are giving your power away. *A sharp tongue can actually cut your own throat!*

Instead of lashing out, analyze those circumstances in life that make you angry. Consider those circumstances a lesson and an opportunity to grow. Underneath anger is a disappointment that the world is not the way you wanted it to be. It's not really what happens in life that upsets you, but the fact that you expected the outcome to be different. Since you are in control of your life, it means that you have created every experience in your life; and, sometimes, you may have created that experience just to learn a lesson. We are all in *Earth School.* The reason you choose that lesson in your life is to learn from it. Sometimes when that lesson becomes painful, you need to be aware of what you're feeling and acknowledge your emotions. As you learn from that lesson, you will learn to choose better; and the results will be better.

Actually, you create your own experiences by the choices you make. When making a choice, it is important, above all else, to acknowledge your feelings. If you don't acknowledge your feelings, you won't identify the real problem. If you can't identify the real problem, you'll mistreat the problem. When you say, *Someone made me angry,* it actually implies that that other person had control over your life. Instead, you should acknowledge the feeling of fear or frustration that the other person's behavior elicited in you— *because you let it happen.* Own your feelings so that you can better understand and control them. Just lashing out at others to express your anger is like picking up a hot coal to hurl at someone who has made you angry. Even if you did manage to hit the other person (which is unlikely), you cannot pick up a hot coal without first getting burned yourself. Since the coal is the hottest when it is picked up from the fire, it is actually *you* who will get burned the most! You need to put the fire out by understanding your own emotions first and then removing the cause of your anger by thinking positive thoughts about the other person or thing. Acknowledge your role in the event, and then take control of your feelings. Just suppressing anger without trying to understand it is like squirting whipped cream over garbage. The result may look good, but the underlying garbage will fester and smell. As a consequence, you'll keep dealing with that same garbage until you get rid of it.

Some people attempt to deal with anger through a process called leveling. When a person is feeling angry, that person is generally feeling inferior to another person because of their own inability to control the situation. Perceiving that the other person is on a higher level and is winning, the tendency then is to try to put that other person down. Sometimes this becomes the only way that the original person feels that they can cope with the situation and will attempt to bring the other person down to their level. However, this reasoning does not work. The other person will get angry about the put-down and will retaliate by putting the originator of the insult down in return. If you are in a situation where you find yourself feeling inferior, it is better to build yourself up mentally, thereby equalizing the levels and regaining control of the situation. Instead of acting in anger and receiving its backlash, you can create the positive results you want by turning the situation around and taking control. Humor helps. If you can make a joke about the situation and laugh at yourself, it eases the tension.

Curbing your anger allows you to focus on what you really want (which is not to make other people angry but to make other people like you). Whenever you walk into a room, if you want to light up that room, be an *energy carrier.* Carry positive energy with you wherever you go. Learn to focus outward. Center your attention on other people in the room, giving them the *triple A treatment*. When you give other people **A**ttention, **A**ffirmation, and **A**ppreciation, you will leave a trail of adoration and affection. Long after you have gone, most people will forget what you had to say; but they will always remember how you made them feel.

Begin with the end in mind. Live your life by focusing on the results that you want. Remember, charm is creative. Anger is destructive to both the carrier and the recipient. Resolve to be resilient. Be like a rubber ball. Just let things bounce off of you. Don't let anger in, or it will fester into hatred. Hated is like a poison that you take with you everywhere you go. Once the poison gets injected into your system, it stays with you and will eventually eat away at your insides. Hatred doesn't hurt the object of the hate. It hurts the carrier! Get rid of hatred and anger so you can focus on fun.

Treat everyone you meet as special, and you will become very special indeed. My all time favorite restaurant in Ocean City is Antipasti because every time I go there, Fausto, the owner, makes me feel so special kissing both my cheeks and escorting me personally to my table. I love to go there not only for the fabulous food, and awesome atmosphere, but also because the owner, who is quite a charmer, makes me feel so good (*Fausto, I love you more!*).

I also have special waiters in my favorite restaurants to whom I give and from whom I receive special attention. They are important to me, and they know it because I ask for them every time I go to that restaurant. In turn, they make every meal a delightful dining experience. At one restaurant, one waiter even used to go out and buy me coleslaw whenever he knew I was coming because his restaurant didn't carry it; and he knows I love it. Another waiter has my drink waiting and a special bread dip. I try to acknowledge everyone in my life such as my masseuse and friend, Alex, for the services they perform as well as the people they are beyond the services they perform. I take an interest in their lives, try to treat them well, and as a result, get excellent service creating happy experiences. It takes a lot less effort to be nice to someone than to be demanding and unpleasant. The results are so much different. I let people know that I care. In return for taking a genuine interest in people, I get special attention, garner priority seating, and feel welcome wherever I go. It's nice to be important, but far more important to be nice!

Be the leader in your own life—not a follower. Develop a strong connection to yourself. In the same way that you might build a relationship with a lover, you can build a relationship with yourself by getting to know yourself first. Learn to accept and love yourself as you are. If you love yourself, everyone will pick up on that cue and love you too. Love emanates from within and radiates without. Base your self-worth on what *you* think of *you*, not on what others think or say about you. After all, who knows *you* better than *you*? Turn self-loathing into self-love. If you don't learn to blow your own horn, no one else will give a hoot! Refuse to settle for anything less than the best, and that is what life will give you.

Love the skin you're in! Look at yourself in the mirror everyday and say kind things to yourself, like, "*I live in a beautiful body, which is a fitting temple for my special spirit. Every day, my body gets better looking as my soul shines from within. I love my beautiful body because I love me.*" Start appreciating your body, part by part. Pretty soon the image in the mirror will conform with your thoughts as you start being defined from the inside. As your outer image aligns with the beauty within, your reflection will glow. The *Mona Lisa* is no more a work of art than you are, so recreate yourself with a smile on your face. Actually, the best dress for any occasion is a happy smile!

Get tuned in, tapped into, and turned on by who you are. When you are in the flow of who you are, you are not bucking the current. Life is easier when you let your inner vibrations create the waves for you. Then you are in harmony with humanity.

Remember who created you, and know that your *DNA is divine!* Honor the supreme being that you are on the inside, but also value whatever form you have chosen to take on the outside.

Just as we love our children, God loves us inside and out or he wouldn't have created us *in his image.*

God doesn't care what you look like, who your ancestors were, how many degrees you have, how much money you make, where you live, or what you do for a living. He just wants to know *who you are* and

when you will get in touch with *who you were meant to be*. Actually, God already knows all of that...
He Is Just Waiting For You To Find Out!

The best thing you can be in life is to be yourself.
Everyone else is already taken!

6

Relationships

God doesn't always give you the people you *want* in your life. He gives you the people you *need*: to help you, to hurt you, to love you, to leave you, to teach you and to help to make you into the person you were meant to be! God sends a variety of people into your life, but you are the one who chooses who will stay and who should go away. Sometimes you just have to know when to let go!

How many of you are just waiting for the right person to come into your life to fulfill you and make you happy? If so far that hasn't happened, let me ask you a question. Why would you put someone else in charge of the most precious thing in your life—like your happiness—when you wouldn't even let another person decide what you're having for dinner or pick out a pair of shoes for you? Why give another person the reins to your happiness by putting that person in control—whether that person wants to be or not? Don't expect someone else to do for you what you can only do for yourself!

How many of you are looking for *your other half* to make you whole and complete? Wouldn't it just be better to become whole on your own and then to find someone else to complement and enhance you? If you go around acting as if you are only half a person, what you will attract is someone else who is only half a person. Together both of you will make up only one person instead of being two separate individuals, who, side by side, could magnify your power ($\frac{1}{2} + \frac{1}{2} = 1$, but a 1 beside another 1 becomes 11). Why not stand side by side and have the power of 11?

Since half a house cannot stand by itself, if your partner (whom you have deemed your other half) should leave, you would crumble and fall. Don't let that happen. Instead, choose to be complete on your own so that what you attract is another *whole* person. The best way to have a good relationship with someone else is to first of all to have a good relationship with yourself. If you have to stop being who and what you are in order to be half of a couple in a relationship, it is not worth it. If the cost to be *half of a couple* is to give up *all of yourself*, then the price is too high. Why give up on yourself as a whole and settle for being half of anything? That kind of relationship will not succeed in the long run. Maybe the people who are always looking to meet *someone special* just need to meet *themselves*!

You see, you don't have to go looking for love in all the wrong places when love is actually right there inside of you. Love is where you come from. Learn to love yourself first and love all of you. Love comes from inside of you, not from outside of you. Feel the love within and let it flow outward.

There's a difference between being alone and being lonely. Human beings are basically social animals. Some of our happiest times are spent with others. If you live in the shell of your own loneliness, you have no one to blame but yourself. Don't be a *Lone Ranger*. Love is all around you once you open your heart and let it in.

The only reason that some people feel lost is that they have not yet found themselves! When you wrap yourself in a blanket of inner happiness, you will always have emotional insulation. Get passionate about yourself first, and then look for another person to share that passion. Surround yourself with people who want to share your passion and want you to succeed.

People come into your life *on purpose, for a season, a reason, or a lifetime*. Partners can come into your life periodically or permanently. There are no accidents in the universe. People choose to come into your life for some reason, and you choose to have them in your life for some reason. If another person wants to be in a relationship with you, and you want to be in a relationship with that person, you are indeed lucky; but only if the union makes both of you happy. Look for the blessing in that union, and the gift it brings to your life. Say, *"It is not just by chance, but by God's great design, guiding both of our steps, that your path crossed mine!"* Relish a good relationship if you have one already. Ask yourself, *"What can I do to make this relationship even better"*, not *"What can my partner do?"*

Happiness is an inside job. Since it comes from within, you are the only one who can create your own happiness. Happiness is a natural state if you don't block it. It is the state in which you were born. Since happiness is a *state of mind*, you can actually choose which state you want to live in. If you live in the state of misery—move! Say *"Mis Ery doesn't live here anymore!"* Only you can control where you live mentally, but you need to be in the right state before you can relate.

Never go into a relationship for the wrong reasons. If you marry or relate to someone for money, you will earn every penny of it, making it the hardest job you ever had. When you marry for money, your marriage becomes a *job* instead of a *joy*. Your job is to constantly please your boss, or you could get fired. Emulating love, if it does not exist, is a very hard thing to do, especially when that love is not heartfelt. Your relationship becomes an economic necessity, but not very fulfilling. No matter how much money your partner has and lavishes on you, you will be selling yourself too cheaply. That's exactly what you are doing—selling yourself. Rather than selling your body and giving your brains away, it is better to sell your brains (get a job) and give your body to someone whom you are crazy about.

Don't end up being a *kept* woman or man. Cattle are kept, animals are kept. People should not be kept. The price of room and board is too high when you have to give up your *self esteem* to get it.

A good relationship should not be a parent-child relationship either, where one partner is always in control and tells the other partner what to do. That does not make the partner who is always being directed and controlled feel very romantic towards their significant other. After all, why would a daughter want to go to bed with her daddy? — Or a son with his mother? Only if the two partners are on equal footing can a relationship be totally fulfilling to both parties.

Never go into a relationship based solely on physical attraction, or *Mr. Right* will soon become *Mr. Right Now*; and *Miss Wonderful* will be *full of wonder* as to when he will call! Physical attraction might be what gets you in the house, but compatibility, communication, and love should be what keep you in a home.

Ladies, do you remember that fairy tale that you believed in as a little girl—the one about growing up and marrying Prince Charming? How did that fairy tale turn out? Are you living happily ever after, madly in love with your fantasy man (you know, the one who wears a cape and can leap over tall buildings)? What kind of life did you picture for yourself when you were a little girl? Surely not one fraught with strife and unhappiness! Whatever happened to that dream of falling in love forever with a Prince Charming who would sweep you off your feet? It's never too late to know!

Take joy in whom you choose to be with, and thank God that you are able to make that choice. In arranged marriages, that is not the case. Many young girls are sold or traded before they even realize that they could have a say in their future. If you're one of the lucky ones who got to choose your own mate, revel in the joy that you are together because you want to be, not because you have an obligation to each other!

A good relationship should enhance your happiness because you are with that special someone who builds you up and doesn't tear you down. To the world, you might just be one person; but to your one special person, you should be the whole world. If your relationship isn't supportive, it is destructive. Marriage should not be about searching and searching only to find that special someone that you want to *annoy* the rest of your life!

A great relationship should be based on a solid friendship that meets the needs of both partners. Whatever qualities you want your partner to have, start by developing those qualities in yourself. The old adage, *If you want to get something, give it away* applies here. If you want to have a good friend, be a good friend. If you want to have love, start by giving love. Think of yourself as being surrounded by all the love and emotion that you want to create for yourself. Then let that feeling emanate from inside of you. Like attracts like!

Companionship and communication are the keys to any great relationship and are even more important than chemistry, although it is wonderful if all three C's exist in a relationship. If you can then create commitment and caring, your relationship will truly be a high five! Start by falling in love with yourself first, then others will fall in love with you. You will know when love is right once you start feeling fulfilled from within and are not just desperately trying to fill a void.

Think from the end. Don't try to get there—come from there, where *there* is a place of total happiness.

The best kind of a relationship is one that brings out the best in both partners, and not one where one partner attempts to capture or own the other. One person can never completely possess another person anyway. To be possessive is to be obsessive. How awful it must be for a person who is possessive to be obsessed with another person. A possessive partner is just throwing his or her own life away by constantly worrying about what their partner is doing. Just as you don't want to be owned because that would make you an object, don't try to own another person. Create happiness when you are together; but do not attempt to smother your partner, and do not let your partner smother you. No one is born to be your keeper. Others may try to guide your behavior toward what makes them feel good, but a great relationship is between two independent individuals, who simply enjoy being together. When your partner is trying to swallow you up or control you, it is not because your partner loves you madly. Rather, it's because of your partners own insecurities. Insecure people need to control everything. They will push and push until they push their partner away. In reality, a partner who is possessive really believes that their significant other is going to leave them anyway because, in their own mind, they never really believed that they were worthy of their partner. A possessive partner always gets to be right in the end because his thoughts are creating not what he wants, but what he thinks will happen.

Find out how to fall in love without losing yourself. Never give up your own identity to be in a relationship that smothers you. The test of a good relationship lies in how well that relationship lets you be yourself without ever having to pretend to be someone you are not. Some people believe that in order to *socialize*, they have to tell *social lies*; but you should never lie about who or what you are in a relationship. If you want to find true love, you have to start by being the true you. Be *self*-conscious. A good relationship should challenge you to seek higher and higher aspects of yourself as both partners grow together and share common goals.

The purest kind of love is to love and to expect nothing in return, but most of us are not that noble. However, needing someone is the quickest way to kill a relationship. Don't be a *cling-on*! Never tell your partner that he would be nothing without you; and, by the same token, don't ever put yourself down or give your power away to your partner. When you say to your partner, "*I was nothing until you came along,*" you are really demeaning yourself and putting too much pressure on your partner to create you. If you make your partner your whole reason for being, you are putting a tremendous burden on him. It changes who he is. Not wanting to let you down, your partner may try very hard to be and do things that are not really consistent with who he is. Your partner then, in essence, is betraying himself to stay in a relationship with you. When your partner can no longer live up to your mental picture of who you want him to be, his resentment will build; and anger will follow. Then when your partner acts in accordance with who he really is, you say that he has changed.

Please allow your partner to be who he is and love him just the way he is. By the same token, if you are married, try not to lose yourself in who your partner is. Wives who play tennis and golf every weekend because it's what their husbands want to do and not really what they want to do are throwing themselves away. Don't lose yourself in a relationship and give up everything you like just to please your partner. A good marriage is one in which each partner has his or her own special interests, friends, hobbies and so on. It is important to not be smothered by your partner, but to just be happy to share his life. It is not your partner's job to make you happy. Your partner couldn't do that anyway, since your happiness has to come from inside of you. All your partner can do is to enhance your happiness once you have found it inside of you. He then has to discover his own happiness as well, which you can enhance. Being true to yourself by holding out for what you think you deserve is what creates a happy interaction with your partner, family, friends, God, and everyone else in the world!

Resolve not to live in anyone's shadow. Live in your own light. I have a very attractive dear friend, who admitted to me that for thirty-five years she lived in her husband's shadow. He called all the shots, made all the decisions, and did exactly as he pleased. My friend didn't even know when her husband was coming home at night. She was supposedly happy living *his life*, but had no control over her own marriage. Then my friend's husband decided he didn't want a shadow anymore and took up with another woman. Actually, that was the best thing that could have ever happened to my friend (although she didn't know it at the time). Once my friend got in touch with her *own power*, she realized that she could sparkle on her own. Suddenly, she came out of the shadows, projecting her own beautiful image and letting others bask in her light. Happily, now that my friend is in control of her own life, she is much better off. Let someone else worry about where her husband is! She is now happy and secure on her own. All of us have that same power— to create who we want to be today (which has nothing to do with who we were yesterday!)

Every one needs to be true to his or herself and not live a lie. You will never have a good relationship based on dishonesty. The only way to be part of a good partnership is to let the other person know who you truly are. If you cannot first love and accept yourself, you cannot expect another person to love and accept you. If you cannot be yourself in a relationship, then the other person doesn't get to know and love the real *you*; and your relationship is based on false pretenses. Don't try to hide your past or mislead a lover by using a lot of smoke and mirrors, because then your lover falls in love with who you aren't. Actually, you are turning your back on *you* when you try to be someone you're not. How can you expect your lover to love you when he doesn't even know who you are? Never rely on a lie. If you want to find true love, start by being the true you. If you don't really like yourself, it will show; and your lover will know.

Retrain your brain! Learn to love yourself first, and then project your own good opinion of yourself. Others will accept your opinion of you because they figure that you know yourself better than anyone. If you think you are worthless and have no respect for yourself, your partner will eventually begin to agree with you. On the other hand, if you think that you are an interesting and worthwhile person, a potential partner will stick around to find out why you have such a good opinion of yourself. Start by asking yourself, *"How do I really feel about me?"* Be confident in the image that you project, because others will accept your opinion of you. After all, who knows you better than you do? What else do others have to go by? Learn to appreciate yourself first and let that self-love radiate from within.

Do you have a *pushover personality?* Putting yourself last in a relationship is definitely not taking care of yourself. Eventually, you will long to be savored. Tell your partner what you want and need. It is crucial in order to have a good relationship that your needs be met. Make yourself important enough so that your needs are met first, and then go on to fulfill your partner's needs. Even on an airplane, a stewardess will tell you to put your own oxygen mask on first because you can't help others without first helping yourself. The most important relationship you will ever have in life is a relationship with yourself. Love yourself first, completely and fully; and then everything else will fall into place. After all, how can there be a *We* in a relationship until there is a *Me?*

Communication is the core of any great relationship. Communication creates caring and commitment. When communication is complicated or has to be secretive because of a third party, it is hard for love to exist. If your relationship has to be kept a secret, you shouldn't be in it!

Your mate may not have a clean slate. When communication between two partners has to be secretive because one is married or there is a barrier to the relationship, it erodes your self-esteem and sense of self worth. Some people choose to be in a relationship with a partner who has a commitment elsewhere and keep hoping that the situation will change. If your partner has to hide and lie about your relationship because of another commitment, think about what that tells you. The truth may be that your partner cannot live up to a commitment period and simply wants someone on the side. By staying in a relationship with a married partner, you are only assuring that the cheater won't leave his spouse. Why should a man, for instance, leave his wife if he can have both of you? A man will generally rationalize and reason that it's cheaper to keep his wife than to pay alimony and child support, especially when he's comfortable in both relationships. When a woman stays in a secretive relationship with such a partner, it only cements the man's thinking that he *can* have both. Don't gamble money you can't afford to lose or risk your heart on someone you can't keep. You will never find happiness when it's based on making someone else unhappy. This is what cheaters do, and cheaters are seldom happy. In reality, they are only cheating themselves because they can't be with the person they really want to be with without having to lie about it.

Check out your partner's history before you start to make history with him. Even if you are lucky enough to finally land your lover, your partner's ex and his kids will all become a part of your life because he is a package deal. But then again, you may be too! Partners should share their history before deciding that they want to make history together. If your partner can't make up his mind about whether he wants to be with you completely and fully, it is better to say no to an incomplete relationship, where you have to share. Keep yourself available for someone who can fully commit to you. Love should feel good. It should not hurt!

If a man is admittedly a player, he will not be a good partner. If a man displays a *Hump And Dump* pattern, *dump the chump*, and find a *champ*! Start by valuing yourself enough to only take up with someone who values you!

Prior to meeting my current husband, I never used to like *nice* guys. To me, they were boring. I always said that I couldn't fall in love unless someone had *bastard* written on his forehead. The bastards were thrilling, but part of the thrill was that they were tear-jerkers. I tolerated their behavior until I learned to value myself and to choose differently. When my first marriage broke up and I was single again, I decided to work on being a *me* before even thinking about becoming a *we*. It took a while because first I had to discover who I was and what I really wanted.

After receiving a double dose of rejection from both my husband and the *friend* he ran off with, I certainly had some ego rebuilding to do. My ego was totally deflated, knowing that I had been played for a fool and had been consistently lied to. All of the hopes and expectations that I had at that time were destroyed. It took me a while to learn to trust again, to dream again, to hope again. However, I found that my dreams became more realistic and actually bigger and better the second time around because I took the time first to find out who I was and what I wanted. I chose to be single for seven years after my first marriage ended. Thank God, I did not relate to another mate because of economic necessity!

Once I got in touch with my own power and established my own identity, I found that I was attracting a different set of men—ones who were secure within themselves and knew who they were and what they wanted. It was really hard for me to trust again; but I found that in order to be happy, you have to trust in something, even if it is just that happiness exists. I looked around at my friends who were the happiest at that time. I noticed that they were all married to *nice* guys. Finally, I decided to give nice guys a try. Then I met a really nice guy, who had enough ornery little boy in him to be exciting. He and I have been happily married for twenty-eight wonderful years, but first I had to learn to value me. By the way, my husband does too! We have a great relationship and totally enjoy just being together.

Conversely, some relationships are so full of bickering that the two partners actually refrain from communicating just so it won't end up in an argument. That kind of relationship does not meet either partner's needs. Peace at any price is no peace at all. If you just go along to get along, you really need to move along. When you're in a dysfunctional relationship with someone else, you're really in a dysfunctional relationship with yourself. Try to create caring instead of aggravating your partner. Collaboration is always better than confrontation. Wouldn't it be better if both of you started cooperating instead of aggravating each other? When you put your partner down or verbally abuse him, it's like saying, *I'm not good enough to have the perfect partner!* Why would you want to live with someone you don't respect?

If your partner doesn't respect you, maybe it's time to replace him with someone who does. Since you teach people how to treat you, ask yourself, *"Why am I teaching my partner to disrespect me?"* Don't allow this to happen. When you learn to value yourself, you will not stay with someone who doesn't value or respect you. Remember, you create what you believe you deserve. If you don't believe you are worthy of love, then you will behave badly or will allow someone to treat you badly, creating results that are consistent with your self-concept.

Once you discover the greatness in you and learn to trust in it, you will tell yourself, *"I now attract only people who treat me in accordance with the greatness in me."* Never abandon your belief in your inner greatness or let anyone abuse you either verbally or physically. If someone should try, don't let their abuse determine who you are or change your state of mind. If your partner does not treat you in accordance with your inner picture of who you are or honor the greatness in you, your partner may not be the right one for you. People who allow their partners to abuse them really suffer from *elf-esteem*, meaning they think little of themselves. These people actually believe that they deserve whatever treatment they're getting from their partners. Unfortunately, their partner may also be suffering from *elf-esteem* and may be looking to build themself up by putting their partner down. React by simply not tolerating any abuse. Walk away from it and resist the temptation to abuse in return. If the abuse becomes physical, walk away and stay away. Once is more than enough for that kind of behavior! Should the abuse become violent, report it to the authorities immediately. No matter how much your partner says he loves you, don't believe him once physical abuse has occurred. Someone who loves you will not hurt you.

Don't worry about destroying the relationship. The abuse has already done that! It's clear that you didn't have a good relationship in the first place, or the abuse would have never occurred. What happens when you refuse to accept the abuse is that you open yourself up for a new and better relationship with someone else, or perhaps even with the same partner, once he has learned to respect you (meaning that he would never verbally abuse you again). To simply tolerate abuse is to ensure it will happen again. If it's physical abuse, again—get away and stay away! Do not accept any apology or condone such behavior. Only a therapist or anger management course could intercede and perhaps make a difference in your partner's life, but it will be hard for you to ever trust him again.

Take the time to get your own life in order. Determine who you are and what you want, and never again allow anyone to abuse you. Again, love should feel good. It should not hurt! If you had to, it would be better to live in a box under a bridge with dignity and self-respect than to allow someone to continually abuse you!

Notice a pattern in the people you attract. Those people showed up in your life for a reason. Since people are your mirrors, ask yourself, *"Are the people in my life praising me, empowering me, and encouraging me to be all that I can be? Am I the beautiful reflection of my love's affection? If not, why not? What is it that I am projecting that makes me not like my reflection in my mirrors or in my partner's eyes?"*

Remember, you can only change one person, and that person is *you!* It is much easier to change what you are doing than to try to change what someone else is doing. Do not act like you are better than anyone else. Just be better than *you* were yesterday. Only compete with yourself, and you will always be the winner!

On the other hand, if you are constantly finding fault with your partner and seem to want to change everything about him, it must mean that you love nothing about him. How can you then say that you love that person? To truly love another person, you have to love most things about that person. Drama in a relationship is caused by power struggles when one partner tries to change the other instead of just loving their partner the way that he is.

Never marry anyone with the intention of changing them. If you dislike everything about your partner, it means you couldn't possibly love your partner; and that means that you really shouldn't be with that person. Maybe you are just kidding yourself about what love is or are creating a fantasy of the other person for you to love.

Learn to love your partner exactly the way that he is. Love the whole person, not just parts of him. I love everything about my husband and wouldn't change one thing about him because then it wouldn't be him. I love every hair on his head (and thank God he still has lots of those!). That's what love is all about.

You can't really change your partner by criticizing what he does or who he is. If you really want your partner to be different, you should find a different partner. When you marry an *apple*, you are married to an *apple* for the rest of your life. You can't change an apple into a pear or an orange. If you wanted a pear or an orange, why did you pick an apple? No amount of paint on the outside is going to change that apple on the inside. Frankly, it's just *bananas* to think that you can change anyone. However, you can help your partner to grow into the best *apple* he can be. If that apple is green, you can help it to ripen and turn it into the most delicious piece of fruit you ever had. But it will still be an apple!

Some people try to use marriage as a panacea or a quick fix for a feeling of emptiness. Never marry someone just to distract you by filling a void when what's missing in your life might just be *you*! A lot of young people just want to get married because they believe that marriage will automatically ensure happiness. After a fairytale wedding though, when happiness doesn't automatically happen, these young people are disappointed. Most of them don't like having to put up with the day to day reality of living with another person, who they thought they knew but didn't. Before making a serious commitment such as marriage, each partner should ask theirself, *"Am I more interested in getting married, with all the hoopla of a big wedding, or in being married?"* Remember, *happily ever after* isn't guaranteed just because two people get married!

Speaking of fairy tales, how many young women actually believe that if they kiss enough frogs, one of them will turn into a Prince Charming? I tried that, but all my frogs turned into were horny old toads until I set out to create my own Prince Charming. I certainly didn't use frogs as the raw material. If you want to *love* happily ever after, make a list of the qualities that you would like your perfect mate to possess. When you finish that wish list of qualities, send that list out into the universe. Be specific in the details on your list, because your thinking actually attracts the physical embodiment of what you're wishing for. Don't skim the shallow waters of a swamp by thinking only of your perfect partner's physical attributes. That's where frogs dwell—hidden under the pond scum. Wish instead for attributes like kindness, understanding, integrity, honesty, intelligence, compassion, a good sense of humor—all the things that make for a real happily ever after. Make sure you throw in a cupful of morals, too. Let the universe package these qualities up for you, while you concentrate on attracting that perfect person to you. Then when your Prince Charming does appear, he will have more substance, and not just be good-looking on the outside.

However, if you choose to stay in the swamp and marry a frog of questionable character (thinking that you can change him), maybe you'd better think again. If that frog has had a history of failed relationships, remember *history does repeat itself*. Don't be taken in by a glib tongue (that's only good for catching flies). Actions speak louder than words. If a person's actions belie his words, say, "*I can no longer hear your words because your actions are ringing so loudly in my ears!*" Select a partner based on actions and intentions and not on lip service. Past behavior is the best predictor of future behavior that I know of. After all, what else can you go by? You can't change your partner's character just because you love him and want to save him from himself. Sooner or later, that person will revert back to being who he is, sometime before he *croaks*.

There's a parallel to this scenario in a parable about a young girl who is walking along the side of the road when, all of a sudden, she sees a foreboding venomous snake.

Surprisingly, the snake calls out to the girl and says: "*Pretty miss, I am so cold lying here in the road. Would you please pick me up and put me under your cloak?*"

The shocked young girl looks at the snake and says fearfully: "*I can't do that because you're a snake, and you might bite me!*"

The snake responds: "*I would never repay your act of kindness in such a way. You can trust me. I just want to get warm. Please, please pick me up."*

The girl, who was very naive and trusting, actually felt sorry for the snake, so she picked him up and put him under her cloak.

Shortly thereafter, the snake bit her! The girl was completely surprised; and, writhing in pain, said to the snake:

"How could you have done that? You promised not to bite me, and I trusted you!"

To which the snake responded: *"But you knew I was a snake when you picked me up!"*

How often are young girls taken advantage of by *snakes?*

Ladies, please be careful, because sometimes a snake can be both a *snake charmer* and a *snake* all wrapped up into one!

In fact, watch out for *poisonous people* period, as they may be very hazardous to your mental health! If a relationship makes you less happy being in it than being away from it, then it's about time to end that relationship. Why pull known toxins into your life that you know are going to make you sick at heart?

How many people, women in particular, have trusted a snake and were surprised when they got bitten? Although I didn't know it at the time, I was one of them. The first time around, I married a real macho male—a good-looking sports jock—thinking that I could turn him into a loving husband and father. Instead, I got bitten! Luckily, I survived and learned to stay away from snakes!

On the other hand, a lot of people live in unhappy marriages and tolerate them, even though they continue to get bitten. Their reasoning is that to get a divorce is to admit failure, but what is successful about living in an unhappy marriage? When you make a choice to change, the world doesn't stamp *D for divorce* on your forehead and make you walk around as if you failed at something.

Wouldn't it be better to be happy alone than to be alone in an unhappy marriage? Endings are painful; but that is the only way for new hope to spring forth, and a new relationship to begin. Since the world is round, sometimes when we come to what seems like the end;

it may only be the beginning. Even what we think of as a dead end could become our *doorway to destiny*. Sometimes a divorce, instead of being a terrible tragedy, can be a thrilling threshold leading to a new and better life. The old relationship must end before a new beginning can blossom. Don't start another relationship until you're out of the unhappy one that you're in. Make sure you finish your current relationship first, or the new relationship will be tarnished by the old.

If you really love your partner, make sure you make every effort to first mend your marriage, if it can be mended. However, if your *spouse is a louse* or a *master manipulator*, and you are only *tolerating* your relationship, why not *terminate* it so that someone terrific can come into your life and elevate it into ecstasy? Not because another person can make you happy, but because you feel so good about yourself when you are with that other person.

First, however, the heart must create its time of snow, and rest in silence, learning to grow. Remember, the most important relationship you will ever have in life is with yourself. You must first nurture the seeds of your own self-esteem into blooms and become the beautiful flower you were meant to be before mating with anyone else in the garden.

If you are just tolerating your current relationship, ask yourself, *"What am I hoping to gain from holding on to this imperfect relationship? Is this relationship providing me security or building on my insecurities?"* Sometimes it is better to just acknowledge that you have learned a lesson and move on. After all, how much drama do you want in your life? If you are in a relationship that keeps you on an emotional roller coaster, it may be time to end the ride. A roller coaster might be exciting for one or two rides; however, I would think a merry-go-round might be better for the rest of your life. You might go up and down a bit, but the ride is always predictable, safe, and happy. People who choose a relationship that is a roller coaster ride, where their heart is always in their throat, will soon get worn out and long for *terra firma*. When that happens, it is time to end the ride. The transition may be difficult for a little while; but you must trust in the future and know that, in the end, it will be worth it.

There are two ways that a marriage can end—either in death or divorce. The death of a cherished spouse can, indeed, be tragic; but sometimes divorce can even be more painful. When your partner dies, you at least have the comfort of knowing that your spouse did not willfully desert you. Coupled with that is the sympathy of your family and friends, in which you can immerse yourself. Never does the thought that your marriage was a failure cross your mind—only the thought of your tragic loss. Instead of living with lawyers and chasing your ex for alimony and child support, you'll find that the insurance company pays up willingly. There is also solace in the thought that your spouse really loved you and left against his will. Further comfort can be found in the belief that one day you will be reunited again— either in the *hereafter* or the next life. You don't have to deal with the problem of being replaced by another person and having to explain that third party to your kids. Jealousy mounts during a divorce when you see that third party actually being accepted by your kids. All of a sudden, you realize that you are being left out of the family you created!

Divorce, especially when there is a third party involved, can indeed be much more stressful than the death of a spouse because of the intense emotions involved—ones that you must cope with on an ongoing basis. Death is tragic but final. There is not the hope that things will change so you don't have your hopes dashed again and again. After a divorce, it might take several years for you to realize that you didn't have a great relationship in the first place, where both partners were fulfilled; or it wouldn't have ended in divorce. A third party couldn't have possibly come between the two of you if the bond between you two had been really tight.

The upside of divorce is that now you are free to find that great relationship that you have always wanted, as soon as you start focusing on yourself and stop worrying about what your ex is doing. When you do find a great new relationship, you will appreciate it even more because you now have a basis for comparison and know how fragile love can be. That great new relationship will definitely be worth it in the long run, once you realize what a great relationship is all about.

A lifelong male friend of mine recently remarked to my husband that he was envious of our relationship because it was obviously a "10." This friend had been married three times; and according to him, the best that he had ever achieved was a "5." Now, after his third break-up, my friend had finally met the perfect woman for him—not only was she beautiful, but she thought he was adorable, interesting, and fun. She also was as crazy about sports as he was. Now his relationship is a "7" and climbing! It made me wonder though, why my friend had ever settled for a "5" and had never before tried to turn his "5" into a "10." Perhaps he didn't know that "10s" existed or didn't think he was worthy of a "10". I hope my friend finds what he is looking for in this new relationship and that he doesn't ever settle for less again. Why settle for less when more is attainable?

Don't stay in a bad relationship because of your children. That is really not fair to the kids, because then they get the job of being a referee while constantly trying to keep the marriage together. Children shouldn't have a job! Ask yourself, *"What kind of a role model do I become for my kids when I settle for less?"* Instead of your children living in a home where two parents respect each other and love flourishes, your kids are subjected to constant battles, teaching them that love is about strife instead of joy and happiness. Children are intuitive and can always sense whether their parents are happy or sad. Actually, children would rather see their parents be happy alone or in a relationship with someone else than living unhappily in a sham of a marriage—all for the kids sake! According to Dr. Phil, "Children would rather be *from* a broken home than to *live* in a broken home," especially when the children think that they are the only glue keeping that home together.

Usually, when unhappy partners separate and find happiness apart, they make better parents. Separated parents actually spend more quality time with their children because they are not being drained in an unhappy relationship or trying to maintain a façade. Very often, when love leaves a marriage before the partners do, one parent may not even want to come home because the nest is nasty instead of nurturing. Think of what that is doing to your children!

You don't have to have a terrible marriage in order to want a better one. You can create a better marriage simply by bringing out the best in your partner. Think of all the things you appreciate about your partner, and tell him regularly. Don't try to control your partner by putting him down. It is better to control with flattery and charm. When you compliment your partner's good behaviors and loving gestures, I guarantee you, you'll get more of those. Would you rather have an ordinary relationship or an extraordinary relationship? If you want a good marriage, create a good marriage. Then pass up good for great, and only settle for more, not less. When your cup becomes full of love, it will spill over and fill other people's cups. It only takes commitment and communication.

When you both enhance each other, it becomes a *joy* instead of a *job* to be with your partner. If, however, the opposite is happening; and your partner is draining your happiness by putting a damper on everything you want to do, it may be time to change partners. Never stay on a relationship that drains you. You may have to put down a *stopper* before you lose your essence, or perhaps it may be time to pull the plug! *If you find you really want out, check out. Just don't sneak out!*

Sometimes we simply outgrow people in our lives, even if they are our spouses, friends, or lovers. Just as you periodically clean out your closet, discarding any clothes that don't fit anymore or have gone out of style, you should discard the people in your life who don't fit the new image or lifestyle that you want to create for yourself. Once you have discovered other people in your life who are more fulfilling and stimulating, the only way you can make room for these new people, who blend in better with your new lifestyle and goals, is to get rid of the old ones, especially the ones who drag you down or hold you back. If your closet is full to the brim with clothes you've outgrown or are out of style, there's no room for new clothes.

Ask yourself, *"How can I create a life that fits who I am now, not who I was?"* Don't worry about all the people from your past who were important to you at one time. There's a reason why they didn't make it to your future. If the people in your life do not support you, stimulate you, excite you, or make your life more comfortable and enjoyable when you are around them, you have outgrown those people. That doesn't mean that the whole relationship was a failure. It's like trying on an outfit that you once loved that just went out of style. You still have the happy memory of how good you looked and felt in that outfit, but now it's time to try something new. Discard an outfit when you no longer feel good about wearing it.

Personally, I have cleaned out my *closet* many times; so that if you are still in my life, it is because I love you and want you there. You and I are a good fit! Remember, never to discard old friends who still feel good to be around. A good friend or partner should be supportive and appreciative of whom you have become and not want to hold you back because he or she can't keep up with you. A good friend will encourage you and want to grow with you. Prize your really good friends—the new and the old. One is silver, the other gold. Never get rid of precious metals!

Lifestyles are also very important in order for partners to be compatible. In between my two marriages, I dated a lot of playboys, who were exciting because of their life styles, which included boating, trips, great meals, concerts, etc. However, what these men didn't value or want to partake in involved things like picnics, playgrounds, little league games, school plays, boy scouts, amusement parks, and trimming Christmas trees, all of which were important to me at that time in my life.

There was actually another man I thought I was in love with when I was single—at least I was in love with his big sailboat and lifestyle of affluence and fun. We dated for two years, and he seemed to love me too! However, although he said he loved me, he didn't love my lifestyle. He once remarked to a friend of mine that I was a wonderful woman, but had too much baggage, referring to my two children and my mother, (who lived with me). Interestingly enough, what I considered my greatest *blessings*, he considered *baggage*; and mine was overweight at that! He constantly compared me to another woman he was dating, who also had two children, but who had lost custody of them to her ex. This woman only saw her children every other weekend, and they were extremely well-behaved because her ex was a strong disciplinarian. I thought my children were well-behaved too because, around me, they were; but my date thought they were brats (although he didn't say so). My children admitted to me years later that they had actually sabotaged this relationship. I was shocked to find out that my children (who thought this man was too old for me) would wait until I left the room to start acting up—throwing food, hitting each other, and so on. When I returned, they were little angels. Their behavior was intended to chase this man away, and it worked (thank you, kids!). This man eventually married a lovely lady with no children, with whom he was more compatible. Then I met my soul mate, who not only gladly carried my *baggage*, he didn't even think it was heavy!

At this point, my kids were either worn out or liked my new boyfriend enough to let him become their dad. Sometimes kids are smarter than their parents, but I would have never married anyone my kids didn't approve of. Actually, my children helped me to pick out my new husband, and we became a family again. One of our first dates alone together was actually a picnic! The good thing was that this man who we picked out together had two daughters of his own and totally liked and understood kids. Our lifestyles meshed beautifully, and I will be eternally grateful to the friend who introduced us (thank you, Ginny!). My marriage has always been fresh and fulfilling; but most of all, it has always been *fun*.

Fun is a key factor in a happy relationship. Play is actually an essential element of love. Ask yourself, *How much fun am I to live with?*

Is your marriage in mothballs? If so, maybe it's time to air it out and put some spring back into it? When you truly love someone, you want that person to be happy and will do whatever you can to enhance their happiness. The other person's job is not to make you happy. No one but *you* can make you happy. Your partner can only enhance your happiness as you do the same thing in return.

Donna, one of my dearest friends (who also has a great marriage) defined the emotional emptiness of her former relationship as *living in a black-and-white world*. However, when she met her second husband, she expressed that her life *turned technicolor*. My husband also *colors* my world, and I adore him. I couldn't imagine going back to black and white, or something would be missing in my life. The quality of a marriage is determined by how well it meets each partner's needs and how much happiness each partner can derive from the union. My husband and I are just simply *better together*, and together is where we want to be. Actually, we're tied together by our heart strings!

A marriage should be about two people, who love each other as much as they love themselves, wanting to constantly bring out the best in their partner, thereby bringing out the best in themselves. A good marriage should grow more divine with time. Don't get married for better or worse. Get married for better, and then make it even better!

Some people think that having a baby might save a troubled relationship and bring the partners closer together. That baby is then born with a job that he is totally unqualified for, which is unfair to the baby. Never trick someone into an unplanned pregnancy, thinking that it will save your relationship. That doesn't work, because then the relationship becomes forced rather than fancied. Relationships can't be forced. They have to be desired by both parties until that relationship becomes the most important thing in both of their lives. A child can enhance a relationship, but should never be used to either heal or seal a relationship.

Marriage should not be a competition. Cooperation is much better than competition for building a strong relationship. When there is competition between the partners, there can only be one winner and one loser. However, when you encourage cooperation, you both become winners; and the union becomes more important than the individual egos. Let go of your need to win if it makes your partner a loser! Why would you want to be married to a loser anyway? When two partners work together, there should be no winners and no losers. Try to turn arguments into a win-win situation for both of you. If you are secure in who you are, you will not need to put your partner down in order to feel better about yourself. Instead, you will respect your partner and his opinion, even if it is different from yours. It is really your relationship with yourself that determines your relationship with others. Respecting yourself is the key to respecting and honoring others.

Let go of your need to be right all of the time. After all, would you rather be *right* or *in rapture* in a relationship? Ask yourself, *"Do I want to be right, or do I want to be happy?"* Instead of acting on a need to be superior to your partner, work on yourself to be a better partner than you used to be. That way you are only competing with yourself, and love stays in your marriage. Your partner can then support you in being the best that you can be instead of wasting time competing with you. In turn, you should support and encourage your mate to be the best that he can be.

Don't look for reasons to be offended by your partner. A very frequent complaint of women in marriages is that their husbands don't spend enough time with them. Between work, sports, friends, regular maintenance on the home, and spending time with the children, sometimes husbands don't have much time left over for their wives. Some wives may feel neglected and will attack their husband the minute he walks in the door, taking out their frustrations on him. This certainly doesn't make a man *want* to spend more time with his wife, especially when she is constantly nagging or complaining. By acting offended or neglected, a wife actually creates the opposite of what she might be trying to achieve. The husband will retaliate by spending even less time with his wife because she is not pleasant to be around, triggering even more resentment on her part. A vicious cycle begins. If a wife really wants to change her husband's behavior to make him want to be with her, she should try to be so charming, interesting, and sexy that her husband can't wait to come home. Any man would want to be around a wife who builds him up and makes him feel special. In return, the husband will make his wife feel special, and the marriage will be so much happier.

Sometimes, it may be the man who feels that the wife is so busy with the children, chores, and housework that she has no time left for him. That man should take the time to discover the *woman in his wife* by helping her to escape the humdrum of daily living by giving her compliments and taking her on a date. If the husband would help with the housework, the wife would have more time for him. Either partner, when feeling neglected or ignored, might be tempted to look elsewhere. Don't let that happen in your marriage. Instead, couples should make time for each other and make plans with each other to escape, even if just for a date night, picnic, or mini-vacation. Too many couples put their relationship on the back burner, when it should be of primary importance. Ask yourself, *What have I done to enrich and nourish my marriage today?* Isn't that what life is all about if you're married? Try creating instead of dissipating.

Put *passion* back into your marriage *on purpose*. Teach your partner how to worship at the fountain of you, and love will just flow! There's no better feeling than spending life with a partner who adores you and is also your best friend. Believe me, I know! Nurture a good relationship, and it will continue to flourish and grow.

If you have all the ingredients for a good relationship, mix them up well, adding a tablespoon of commitment, a cup of communication, and two quarts of love. Bake the batter in a warm, nurturing atmosphere. If your cake turns out perfectly, savor it, and enjoy it every day. Don't throw a good cake away when it gets a little stale. Sprinkle it with little moisture drops of understanding and devotion, and that cake will be as fresh as it ever was. Instead of throwing away a good cake, remember that it took so long to bake; and you may never have that recipe again! Savor a good relationship by enjoying your cake every day. A good relationship should be your *just desserts*. It should be sweet, taste good, and make both of you happy in the consumption.

Occasionally, turmoil will erupt in any marriage, mostly because of pent-up emotions. The most terrible thing that can happen in a marriage is not the occasional bickering or even constant fighting, although both can be self-demeaning and disruptive. If you temporarily hate your mate, at least it shows that your passion is still alive. Love and hate are both passions; but one is constructive, and the other destructive—destroying both the sender and the receiver. Open the lines of communication before you get to the state of hating your mate. Talk about your feelings and what it is that is really bothering you. Remain in the moment. Do not bring up the past or other people. Tell your partner exactly how you're feeling in the moment and why. Communicate your feelings clearly as they occur and before they become magnified. Wanting to rush home to tell your partner about your day is a much better feeling than dreading to walk in the door.

I remember a very attractive female friend of mine (who was the main breadwinner in the family, but whose marriage was breaking up) telling me that she used to walk three miles around her neighborhood at night before she could get up the courage to walk in her own front door. It was because she dreaded the confrontation that awaited her on the other side. What a terrible feeling—to *dread your own door* because of what lies inside! That is just the opposite of what your home base should be. Your home should be like what a charger is to a cell phone—the place where you go to have your life energy renewed and your batteries recharged. If you can't plug in to positive energy at your base, your battery will soon wear down; and you will not be receptive to any signals. If you cannot let your feelings out, your system will go on overload. Then you will shut down emotionally.

Ironically, the most dangerous point in a marriage is not when you occasionally hate each other. The most dangerous point in a marriage is when you become *indifferent* to each other and stop talking, sharing, and caring. When you reach that point, it signals the death of the relationship. Just like having a dead battery, all communication shuts down.

When you can no longer receive or give out signals, your power is gone. Once that happens, you either need to plug in (if you care enough to do so), or to seek a new base. Only when you can walk out the door with emotional peace and no anger or hurt feelings, only when you can leave with less than apathy, will you know that the relationship is over. When you can say to yourself, *"I did everything I could, but this marriage isn't working,"* it is the time for you to find fulfillment on your own. Actually, it may also be the time for you to *eat, drink and remarry!*

Don't stay in a marriage where both of you are the reflection of each other's resignation. Get back to spousal arousal if you can, and make your marriage your mission. If the candle of passion has flickered and gone out temporarily—so what? You have a piece of flint and a spark! If you really have the desire to get the fire back into your marriage, rub the flint and spark together; and you will soon have a glowing ember, again. Keep trying to ignite each other until the fire of passion burns brightly— if you think that there is something there worth salvaging.

Don't act like you don't care. Marital disinterest cuts to the core of your soul and will slaughter it if left unopposed. Most people want to live in a home not just a house. Your home should be a happy haven, your *soft place to fall*, where you get renewed each day with a high dose of loving, supportive energy. My home and my marriage are like that. I can't wait to hear my husband's footsteps walk in the door. A day without him would be like a day without sunshine. We can live together in loving harmony twenty-four hours a day and still be best friends, mutually supporting each other's goals. There is no one I would rather be with. Both of us want nothing more than for the other to be completely happy and fulfilled. My husband has totally supported all of my dreams—most recently, the one to write this book, which he has patiently typed up for me— a myriad of times! Likewise, I have supported my husband's dream of finding and restoring a 1959 Cadillac convertible. This dream of his has involved a lot of time and money, which many women might object to. However, that's his dream, and he supports mine. That's what a good relationship is all about!

My first marriage wasn't like that. I married a mirage of the man I wanted my husband to be, and I suppose he married a mirage of who he wanted me to be. I don't think either one of us knew the real person underneath. His image married my image based on physical attraction and little else of what was really important like common goals, communication, or values. When my first husband ran off with my friend, my soul actually breathed a sigh of relief, even though my heart was angry and sad. Actually, it wasn't until I lost my ex that I found me! I was trying to project onto my ex the lifestyle that I wanted, which involved kids, family, friends, and a house in the suburbs; but he rejected my visions. I guess that just wasn't him!

My ex was extremely handsome and well-built when I met him; and although I hate to admit it, the first time around I married mainly on physical attraction. This might have been enough for me at twenty-three, if I had not hoped for more and just assumed that it would be there. That marriage was like receiving a beautifully wrapped present and excitedly opening it up only to find a whole different present on the inside than what had been hoped for. When it turns out that the present on the inside is not something that you want or even like, the wrapping on the outside really doesn't matter. I just kept hoping that I was wrong, and kept looking for a real present in there somewhere!

I realized much later that the real present was my ex's exit, which gave me back my freedom. It took a while for this realization to sink in. At first, I just wanted my ex to live up to his responsibilities and to at least be a father. I had a court order for child support which he paid for a while; but since my ex moved from state to state, it was very difficult to catch up with him to collect the money when he didn't. I was having a hard time mentally swallowing all of this because my ex's abrupt departure had shaken my values to the core. I had always believed that life should be fair. Just like in the movies, the good guys should win, and the bad guys should lose. However, I came to realize that sometimes it just takes a little while for that to happen, and that one has to *manage in the meantime.*

I was totally shocked by what my ex-husband did and with whom he did it! The whole thing was hard for me to comprehend. In my mind, the other woman certainly wasn't an upgrade! Finally, the realization set in that a partner doesn't always leave you *for more.* Sometimes they leave you *for less* so that they *can feel like more!* What I was viewing as a loss was really just a lesson. What had I lost? Only a man who had *pretended* to care about his family and a *faux friend!*

I finally realized that my friend actually did me a big favor by taking my ex off my hands. Both of them were exactly alike, just two people who showed by their actions that they could care less about anyone else—including their own children! They deserved each other! If what they did was in accord with who they truly were, I certainly would not want to be married to that kind of man for the rest of my life nor to have that kind of woman for a friend!

I just had to get over the shock of finding out that who these two people really were was not who I thought they were. When my husband ran off with my friend, took all the money in our bank account, and even borrowed against my life insurance policy, I was floored! I had no clue that my husband was even having an affair (which he knew I would never have tolerated). The worst part was to discover that my ex was moving out-of-town and totally turning his back on his kids. The other woman was also doing the same thing to her kids (a boy and girl, aged 10 and 12), and her husband of fifteen years. I had lived with my husband for ten years and thought I knew him, but obviously I didn't! The man I thought he was could have never done what he did. Not only did my ex choose to hardly ever see his kids after he left, he also tried to absolve himself of all financial obligations for their support and mine. My ex's actions actually shook me to my core because he had violated my values. I had always believed that daddies did not depart, spouses should not cheat, and good friends would not stab you in the back! I never dreamed that any mother would voluntarily leave her kids for any man, and I always believed that parents should at least live up to their financial responsibilities! My beliefs were broken! I had a hard time realizing that my husband, whom I had loved and lived with for ten years, could turn into a person I didn't know, or worse yet, didn't even want to know. Unfortunately, I had married the person I thought he was, *not* who he was. If *who he was* was really the person he turned out to be; I would have never chosen to marry him. Even in my naive years, I would have wanted someone with more integrity.

I was even more shocked by my ex's actions because he had come from a broken home and always swore that he would never do to his kids what was done to him. My ex's father had run off with his mistress after ten years of marriage, leaving his wife and two boys. My ex had experienced the pain that this could cause a child. Actually, there was a time when my ex's father had both his mistress and his wife pregnant at the same time. His father chose to be with his mistress, although he did support his boys and maintained contact with them. My ex's mother (who had a miscarriage after she found out what was going on) threw her wedding ring off a bridge as a symbol that their marriage was over. Unfortunately, this was my ex's history. I guess patterns really do repeat themselves. I wouldn't have believed it, though, because during our marriage, my ex was so adamant that he would never cheat or put his children through what he had gone through. Thank God, my son has not followed this pattern. But then, he was not raised by his father!

What a revelation it was when I finally realized that the worst thing that I could ever imagine happening in my life turned out to be the best thing that could have happened! What was I so upset about? My image of my ex was shattered, but that was obviously not who he really was. After the divorce, I did miss the man I *wished* I had been married to, but not the man I *had* been married to. Actually, I was just mourning the *loss of a dream!*

Now I was free, but I had two small children who were totally dependent on me. In reality, though, I was the lucky one—I got the kids, the house, the mortgage, the car payment, and all the bills; but at least I was guilt-free and had my integrity. My ex got all the collectable cash, but also all the guilt.

Actually, I came out way ahead! The sad part, though, was that my *macho* ex-husband couldn't even be *man enough* to tell me what was going on. I would have respected him a lot more if he had at least been honest with me. When my friend's husband called to tell me that my husband was running away with his wife, I thought it was a bad joke and hung up on him—twice! To me, it was unbelievable that I actually had to find out from my friend's husband that these two *mature* adults were running off together to another state and that they were leaving his children, her children, both spouses, her teaching job in mid-term, and all their responsibilities behind. This speaks volumes about the type of people they were; and, thank God, they are no longer in my life! It was quite a lesson; but for the rest of my life, I learned to choose better. That's when my life got better and better.

My first inclination was to chase after my ex to make him pay until I realized that I was just throwing myself and my money away. Actually, it turned out that my ex-husband's leaving was the best thing that could have ever happened to me! I got to discover *who I could be.* Since I had always believed that the man should be the one to succeed, I had spent a lot of time and effort trying to make that happen, even though I could always outsell, outshine, and outperform my ex-husband on any mental task. Perhaps that was part of his problem, although while we were married, he had achieved success as a manager and supervisor of health clubs, a business I had brought him into. After eight years of working for the health club, I had finally felt comfortable enough financially to give up my job and to just do some substitute teaching so I could be home with our kids. I had just begun to dabble in real estate when I got the shock of my life. Obviously, my heart was not in real estate at that time.

However, once I stopped chasing my ex for support and even caring about what he was doing, I was able to change my focus by putting my whole self into my real estate career and into raising my two children. I had just started in real estate when my ex left and had not made one penny in income; but at least I had *me*! I quickly learned that if I was going to survive, it was up to *me* and *me* alone. The seas were rough, but I had two small children on my back; and I certainly was not going to let them drown. Thank God, I also had my mother, who, although she couldn't help me financially, moved in with me to help take care of my children. (Thank you, Mom!)

I went to work equipped with my *victim story*, thinking that sympathy would sell houses. But that didn't work! I quickly found out that people wanted to buy houses from a *victor*, and not a *victim*. The only person who was making me a victim at that point was *me* because I had chosen to stay in that role rather than taking control. Gradually, I started to study success to learn about the habits of people who were successful. During my first six months in real estate, I didn't sell anything. That was the time when my creditors were going to take my house and my car and shut off my electricity!

There was even a time when my manager at work wanted to fire me because of my lack of production. He hesitated to do so only because he knew what I was going through. When that manager hired me, he had thought that I would be a hot shot sales agent (given my history of being the top salesperson for the health club, where I had worked previously). Fortunately, my manager didn't have the heart to just let me go. Instead, he suggested that I take a psychological test to determine what field I would best be suited for (thinking that he could use those results to suggest that I go back to teaching). However, the results of that test clearly stated that *this person would do extremely well in a people-oriented sales business*— like real estate. Based on those test results, my manager decided to give me another chance (thank you, Rich!).

Because of a change of attitude during my second six months

in real estate, I settled a million dollars in volume my first year—which was quite something thirty-eight years ago. The rest is history! Subsequently, I became Coldwell Banker's number one international agent. In the late nineteen-nineties, I actually settled over a hundred million dollars in volume in one year—mainly because I stopped being a victim, took charge of my own life, and got in touch with my own power!

My kids, by the way, have also turned out wonderfully, despite the fact that I was a single, hard-working mom for seven years before the love of my life came along. This man and I have been together for more than thirty of the happiest years of my life. My children have both decided (on their own) that they wanted nothing to do with their biological father, but are very close with both my husband and I. What a loss for their former father, who is now nothing more than a sperm donor!

It looks like the good guys do win in the end! I became so much better off in the long run— excelling in a career in real estate (that I would not otherwise have had), raising two wonderful children (who are a big part of my life) and being married to a man I adore. On the other hand, I could have stayed wallowing in self-pity, drowning in debt, or reeking with revenge. Instead I chose to be *happy*. Our choices make all the difference in life! Once I learned to value me, I ended the cycle of picking problem partners by choosing a man whose values and morals were consistent with my own.

My ex-husband pulled the rug out from under me, taking whatever economic security I had since I was hardly working at the time. However, instead of falling on my face, I created a new rug—a magic carpet that responded only to my voice and took me wherever I wanted to go. I never relinquished the control of my rug after that. It took me a long time to learn to trust again and to let anyone on that carpet with me! Now my current husband (whom I totally trust) can be on my magic carpet with me anytime since we share the same dreams and want to go in the same direction.

I have found that the most important element in a marriage is *trust*. In the middle of the word trust is an "*us.*" In order for there to be an "*us,*" *trust* must exist. It is the single most important ingredient in a relationship. The worst thing you can lose in a marriage is your partner's confidence and trust in you or your trust in him. Without trust, even a dream marriage can become a nightmare, especially when one spouse feels compelled to question their partners every move by constantly checking e-mails, cell phone calls, and monthly credit card statements. Behaving in this manner transforms a person from a partner into a paranoid parent! If you have to keep your spouse on a short leash, it may be better to let him go. Otherwise, you will choke him. Better to let your partner run free, so you will know that when he chooses to walk with you, it is because he wants to be by your side. Hopefully, your spouse is trustworthy because of who he is and not because you are checking up on him.

Suspicious minds are never happy minds. Living with suspicion is no way to live happily ever after with another adult. Each partner should be trustworthy in a relationship, not because their partner might be checking up on them, but because of their own integrity and desire to do so. In order to be able to trust someone else, you have to be trustworthy yourself.

The *measure of a man* is not how many women he can seduce, but how many ways he can make one woman happy, who in turn will make him happy. Trust is of paramount importance in that kind of relationship. Hopefully, that trust will never be betrayed.

True love is like having a fine piece of crystal, that should be cherished. If that crystal gets broken, even once, you can pick up all the pieces and glue them back together; but you will forever see the cracks. Subject that same piece of crystal to any heat, and it will all fall apart again. Keep your crystal intact, and cherish it like the fine, rare piece that it is!

Life can be so wonderful with the right partner, but sometimes it has to start with the right partner for you being *you*! The purpose of searching for a relationship is not to find another person to complete you, but to find another person who can share in and compliment your completeness. Start by being self-centered. You can never truly fall in love with another person unless you are in love with yourself first.

Have you noticed a pattern with your partners? Do your

relationships always end up the same even though they involve different places and different faces? Are you living the same relationship over and over again? Think about your patterns and why they are perpetual. Who is perpetrating them? Maybe its time to make a change. If you don't like the kind of fish you're catching, you need to change your bait!

Why is it that we will fight for the person who wants to leave us and ignore the people who truly love us? There comes a point in our lives when we should realize who really matters, who never did, who won't anymore, and who always will. The people in your life who care will always be there; and those who don't, won't! Eventually, you will discover the difference between *friend and faux!*

Pass up living in a *pity pot*, by realizing that you are in control of your own life. If you betray yourself by completely giving yourself away in a relationship, you will feel less happy in that relationship than you would feel by yourself. A relationship should be an opportunity to create the highest actualization of yourself— not to lose yourself, and certainly not to control another person, who should be seeking the highest actualization of himself. True love should make your heart sing. Summon all the joy you can within that song. Try feeling completely in love for a day—even if the person you are in love with is you!

A person who truly loves you will want to spend his or her life ensuring your happiness and not putting you down. If your partner is constantly berating you by calling you names, the real reason that he is acting that way may be that he is feeling inferior or unloved himself. Instead of responding to insults in anger and calling your partner names in return, try stroking your partner verbally and building up his ego (which is something he cannot seem to do for himself). Do not accept your partner's verbal insults as the truth about you. Recognize them only as your partner's calling out in need for more stroking or acceptance. If your partner were drowning, you would not be telling him how stupid he was for falling overboard, would you? Help your partner. Do not fight back or engage your partner on an anger level of name calling. That will simply fuel the fire of his anger and lower you to his level.

Try retaliating with humor. Deflect anger with a shield of humor by refusing to be insulted. When your partner realizes that his tactics are not upsetting you, as he had intended, he will stop. One of the worst things my current husband has ever said to me was, *"I think you could have used another hour of sleep this morning."* That was a polite way of saying I was acting like a bitch that day, and it made me angry, at first. However, when I thought about it, if that really was the worst thing he ever said, I was lucky. I could have responded with *"How dare you insult me, you bastard!,"* and an argument would have ensued. Instead, I responded with *"You'll do anything to get me in bed, won't you?"*

Humor deflects insults, which then have no impact. When you demean your partner or put him down by calling him names in return, he will remember those names long after the issue has passed. Do not engage verbal insults with more verbal insults because that is like pouring gasoline on a fire. It will result in an explosion.

Partners can fight all they want, but no mental or physical beating will ever bring a lover back to you. The only beating that will ever make anyone love you is the beating of his or her own heart. Love is a feeling that can be instilled, but it can't be beaten into anyone. You can't force someone to love you. If you want love in your life and do not have it now, try to creatively visualize the perfect partner for you. Put into that visualization all the qualities you would like to have in a partner without giving that partner a face. Then say in your visualizations, *"The perfect partner for me now appears ...,"* and let the universe take care of the details.

You cannot visualize that anyone in particular, say "Tom," loves you as much as you want to be loved, because that would be controlling Tom. That might not be what Tom has in mind or what the universe has in mind for you or Tom. Just be open to the possibilities, and the right partner will come along. It might even be Tom, but you are creating the right partner for you and not controlling Tom. In the meantime, you should be developing the qualities in you that such a perfect partner might want in his mate. Since like attracts like, develop in yourself all the characteristics that your perfect mate might find attractive; and then let that perfect partner find you. For instance, if you want a person with depth, start by developing depth in yourself. A person with depth would not relate to a shallow mate.

How can you tell if your partner is really into you? The message is on their face. Some people try to mask their emotions, but faces and expressions don't lie. Of all the things you can wear, your expression is the most important. When you learn to listen with your heart and read faces (as I have), you will hear what isn't being said. Three faces of friends of mine, who were going through intense emotions at a certain time in their lives, really stand out in my mind. Their faces said it all!

First of all, on the face of a dear male friend, there was the *look of love*. This look was so obvious when my friend was with the woman he adored (although he had not yet left his wife). His face just lit up with a smile from ear to ear every time he looked at the object of his affection. Love just oozed out of his eyes. He was alive in the anticipation that he and his sweetheart would soon be together permanently as a couple. Although these two lovers had not yet announced their intentions, there was no hiding the love on my friend's face. It was exhilarating to see and feel his joy.

The next day, I went to a luncheon and saw a different look on another friend's face. I call it the *look of loss*. My friend's wife had been diagnosed with terminal cancer, and she had taken a turn for the worse. Sadness was written all over his face—from the blank stare to his down-turned lips. He looked like a man who wanted to cry but couldn't. I could have cried for him, but it wouldn't have eased his pain. (His wife passed away shortly after that. Now he has learned how to celebrate her life and not her death.)

A few days later, I went to a party and saw yet another look— perhaps the most poignant of them all. I call it the *look of longing*. This look was on a very attractive female friend's face. She was stuck in an unhappy marriage, where the embers of love and respect had died out; and she was longing for romance to return to her life. Without my friend saying a word, I could read the nostalgia in her eyes where memories of love had been. Resigning herself, because of her four children, to stay in a marriage where love no longer lived, her face said it all. A longing for what might have been was written all over it. I don't know if she will ever have the courage to initiate any change, so her eyes will continue to have that faraway look. What a shame! When will her longing be replaced by love?

What look is your face wearing today? Looks can't be masked with make-up! They are the messengers of what is going on inside.

Hopefully, you can put on a happy face by creating a relationship that you really want to be in, not one that you are simply tolerating. A person should never have to beg for love from anyone.

Don't be a victim of emotional rape or emotional blackmail by letting someone else play with your emotions. If someone is playing with your heart by constantly plucking your heartstrings, you may have to cut them, as painful as that may be. An obsession with another person is what causes a relationship to fail. When you become totally focused on another person and forget who you are, you won't find fulfillment. Focus on yourself first and try to discover the cause of your own unhappiness. You can leave a relationship because you are unhappy, but it will still be an unhappy person that you are taking with you. Since you take *you* with *you* everywhere you go, you have to concentrate on making *you* happy first. Just because you are not a perfect match for your current partner, it doesn't mean that there is anything wrong with either one of you. There may just be a better match for you in your future, as well as a better match for your partner. You may have not connected on all levels with that one partner, but the perfect partner for you does exist.

Remember, your DNA is divine. We are all sons and daughters of God. If your present partner doesn't believe in you and encourage you, then you need to find someone who will. Start by ending your current rocky relationship first. Cheating while in a relationship never creates contentment. It only creates chaos. Cheating is actually a choice. It doesn't just happen. Sometimes, there can be a *rocky road* between *banana splits* and *splitting assets*, but you have to finish with the old business first before something new and delicious can come into your life. Your choices will be much clearer if you end the old relationship first, rather than taking up with another partner while still in the *fog* of the old relationship. When you cling to the cushion of trying to find another partner first because you are afraid to be alone, it certainly limits your choices. Any worthwhile, self-respecting person with values will not choose to begin a relationship with a person who is committed elsewhere. Therefore, while you are in such a vulnerable state, you could be taken in by trash!

People who have nothing to hide, hide nothing. People who cheat and lie about it think they won't ever get caught. That is a fallacy. These people are not living in the real world, but instead are living a lie. It's not really who you *lie with* that's important, but who you have to *lie to* to do it that matters. Why can't a person who intends to cheat just be honest with everyone, including himself, and make the real world coincide with his fantasy? The problem is that most cheaters don't know what they want; therefore, they can never achieve true happiness with any one person. Instead, cheaters just go on hurting others until those others get smart and demand more for themselves. No partner is worth crying over because if he were, he wouldn't make you cry. If your partner can't be monogamous and honestly tells you so, then you need to decide if you can accept being in a relationship with half a person. If you can't, then go out and find a whole person, knowing that you're entitled to more!

Multiple partners never multiply the joy in a relationship, only the pain. Monogamous relationships should double the joy and divide the pain. If you are sharing your partner with another, you are only getting half of what you should be getting. It is even more important, though, to recognize that you don't have the right to destroy someone else's family, especially where there are children involved.

When a relationship begins with deception, there will always be an issue with trust. *If he'll do it with you, he'll do it to you!* There's a difference between *love* and *lust*. Expect more from your partner. Expect *a real relationship*. It is too much pain to bear when you have a partner that you have to share!

Loving someone should never be about getting revenge. If you're looking to get even because you have been hurt, or to make your partner miserable because that's how you're feeling right now, that is not love. If you have been hurt, ask yourself, *"Do I really want to get even, or do I just want to get over it?"* The best revenge against someone who has hurt you is to simply remove that person from your life. Move on so you can be happy with someone else.

Instead of moving on, some people choose to get on a *bus bound for Bitterness.* Why would anyone choose to ride that bus? It is not a pleasant ride, and you certainly will not enjoy the other passengers on the bus who are all moaning and groaning. You will not even like your destination when you get there. There is nothing to see or do when you arrive in *Bitterness,* except to be bitter. Once you get there, it takes a long time to get a return bus back. It is better to pass up that bus bound for *Bitterness* and to hop on the one headed for *Happiness.* Choose to get *better,* rather than being *bitter!* Instead of concentrating on what could have been, concentrate on what could be. When you spend your life trying to get revenge on a person who has hurt you, it only extends the hurt you are going through. Revenge is a boomerang that comes right back to you, and you can't heal if you keep throwing darts at your own heart. Trying to hurt the person who hurt you just doesn't work. Obviously, that person doesn't care, or he wouldn't have hurt you in the first place. However, when the person who hurt you sees you happy with someone else, that person may have second thoughts. It is better to let that other person eat his heart out while you are happy with someone new. Any negative emotion felt by that other person then will boomerang back to him and won't hurt you.

While it is normal to feel intense anger when going through a divorce, especially if there is a third party involved, you can handle the rejection and dejection by learning to love yourself and accepting what you cannot change. The only things that you can change are your expectations and your reactions. Learn to handle yourself with emotional integrity without panicking, falling apart, or being filled with fear. Actually, the end of something can become the beginning of something new and exciting when you learn to celebrate life through both its pain and its pleasure. Stop playing a victim. Take charge of your life, and let God clear out the clutter. (I didn't realize that was what God was doing in my life until later.)

When my first marriage broke up abruptly and painfully, I wanted all the sympathy I could muster from friends and acquaintances to soothe me. What I realized later though, was that their sympathy was smothering me and keeping me from healing. Counting on your friends to commiserate with you during a divorce may not be the wisest thing to do. Actually, it keeps you mired in misery because you are dwelling on it. When I was going through a painful divorce and was full of anger, I remember that only one of my friends said, *"Get over it! Get on with your life. You are more than the way you are acting."* I thought that was a terribly cruel and callous thing to say at a time when my heart was breaking, and I actually became angry at my friend for saying it. Later I realized that it was the kindest thing she could have said.

If you want to effect change in your life, start making different choices, but remember to learn from the lessons of the past. Ask yourself, *"What kind of strength have I gained as a result of this experience? How can I use this strength in a positive way when relating to someone else?"*

There's power in pleasure. Take your power back by pursuing your own pleasure. Put yourself in charge of your own happiness. Don't make your *someday isle* an *island of regret*.

Live fully in the moment and be in love with life. Don't be tempted by the wrong person. Patterns do repeat themselves! Past history doesn't always determine future behavior, but what else can you go by?

When you learn to choose better, you will do better! If your partner cannot make a commitment to you without feeling like he is committing himself into an institution (which is, after all, what marriage is), then that person should not make a commitment at all. Sometimes partners are commitment-phobic because they have been hurt in a previous relationship or lack the belief that relationships can last. Some people may even think that the way not to get a broken heart is to pretend not to have one at all! However, these people are also denying themselves all the joy that a happy heart can hold. Instead of a commitment, marriage should be a *communion* between two souls, who vibrate in harmony with each other, realizing that they are happier together than they could ever be apart. Neither partner should pressure the other for a commitment, but each partner should just relish their joyous union as it expands and becomes all encompassing.

You can't mandate love; you can only motivate it,
enrich it, nourish it, and then let it flourish!

7

Parenting

One of the most important relationships you will ever have in your life (if you are blessed enough to have another soul entrusted to your keeping) is with your child. Being a parent means you have been selected by another soul to be its *shepherd* and are in charge of protecting it, feeding it, loving it, and leading it for a little while. To that young soul, you are a hero who can do no wrong. Children emulate their parents' actions and pick up on their words. Parents are the most important role model in a child's life, so parents must take that role very seriously. If your children love you, they will want to grow up to be just like you. That is an awesome responsibility!

Why then would you model behavior in front of your kids that is the opposite of what you would want them to learn? You can tell a child, "*Do as I say, don't do as I do*"; but they will do as you do if they really love you. Kids absorb you. Initially, all they want to do is to be with you and try to understand you. Don't ever lie to your children about what you're feeling. Explain to them why you are feeling the way that you are so that they will know whether or not it has anything to do with them.

Never put a child down for asking questions. That is how a child learns about life. Help your child seek out answers to his questions if you don't already know the answers. Sometimes those answers may actually lie within the child himself. That might be why your child asked the question in the first place to verify the answer that is within him. Help your child to find the answers that are true for him so he can make his own decisions and not be affected by bad influences. Children mimic what they see others doing, whether it's on TV or in real life. Children emulate what they are entertained by, even if it's violence, sex, or drunken behavior. Where do children learn about such things? From the TV, of course, which many parents use as a built-in babysitter!

Kids don't come with an owner's manual or operating instructions, so you have to fall back on your own instincts. Children should be considered a blessing in your life and never a burden. Treat them like the blessings that they are and show them how happy you are to have them.

Many parents will raise their children the same way they were raised—whether it was right or wrong. Examine the results of your upbringing. Those results will determine whether it was right or wrong. Are you a happy, loving, independent individual, or are you a byproduct of the blame that you heaped on your parents? You can't change your upbringing now, but you don't have to repeat it. *Rise above your raising!*

A child is just a child for a little while; but somewhere, within that child, the manuscript for the man is being formulated. The most powerful role model in a child's life is the same sex parent, and the opposite sex parent is a very close second. Whether a parent is good or bad, a parent will always be a hero to their child, a hero that that child looks up to and depends on. Therefore, parents should always keep their word and fulfill any promises made to a child, not just because they don't want to let their child down, but because they want to keep their image of being a hero intact.

Praise is much better than punishment for controlling and disciplining your child. Rewards always work better in creating a desired behavior. You will get a much better performance from a child by giving him attention and praise instead of a scolding or a put down. Don't bring your child up by putting him down! Remember your child is an extension of you. A put-down from the most important person in his world stays with a child for a very long time. It takes more than fifty *atta boys* to erase even one put-down from a parent. Do not deal with a child by showing your disapproval or being sarcastic. Instead, when you want to motivate good behavior in your child, find out what his currency is. What does your child value? Is it toys, video games, TV, cell phone time, or your time and attention? Trade your child the things that he values as a reward for his good behavior. That way your child can earn what he values the most and get paid in his own currency. Bear in mind that a child's most important currency really is your approval, and he will trade anything to get it. You can take away your child's toys if he misbehaves, but don't take away your love. Never turn your child's *upbringing* into a *down-bringing*. It is very important for you to believe in your child until he can learn to believe in himself. All a child really wants from his parents is to know that he is loved and accepted, no matter what! Isn't that what nurturing is all about?

Children will seek attention and positive reinforcement for their good behaviors first. However, when they don't get it, children will often exhibit bad behavior to get the attention they crave. Never reward bad behavior. One way not to reward bad behavior is to pretend that it doesn't exist. When your child is having a temper tantrum, just walk away! You can also use humor and say *"That was a pretty good tantrum. Can you do it again?"* That way a child learns that a tantrum only provides a temporary diversion and doesn't get him the results that he wants. Never reward a tantrum by giving into your child's demands, or he will exhibit that behavior repeatedly. (Hey, it works!)

Don't yell at your child. Yelling doesn't work. It just signals to your child that his behavior is getting to you by making you lose control. What a child learns when you yell at him is to yell back; and all of a sudden, you're in a screaming match with the person you're supposed to love the most. Try *whispering* to your child instead of yelling. The child will have to actually stop screaming or doing what he is doing to hear what you are saying. To be even more effective, get down on your child's eye level and whisper. That way you are modeling good behavior to your child, all the while showing him that you are in control. The child will then learn that his bad behavior has not gotten to you as he had intended.

External validation is very important to a child and remains so until he is old enough to learn how to validate himself. At times, children will, of course, do things that you don't like—after all, they're children! If a child acts up in a negative way, that child is just looking for attention and is asking for boundaries to be set. Actually, what every child needs is *love and limits*. Limits have to be set by the parents and enforced by the parents. A child may test those limits; but when his boundaries are consistently reinforced, the child will eventually learn to set up his own *invisible fence*.

Never put a child down personally for bad behavior. Make the behavior wrong, but never the child! Don't tell a child that *he* is *bad*, only that his current behavior is unacceptable. Divorce the child from his actions so that he does not label himself as *bad*. Tell your child how wonderful he is and that you expect better behavior from him than what he is currently exhibiting. Say, "*I love you, but I don't like what you did*." Make your child realize that a particular behavior does not suit him because he is much better than the way he is acting.

Give your children *self-esteem shots!* Build up your child's self-esteem so that he will want to consistently live up to your good opinion of him. Never tell your child that he is a bad child, or worse yet, how stupid he is. Don't ever *label* children. Children will live their labels. *Labels are lethal* to a child's self-image, which is formed at an early age. When a child is linked to a label, he will continue to act out that label for the rest of his life because of the improper self-image that he has created as a result of that label.

Let your child know how special he is to you and what your expectations are of him. Applaud him each time he lives up to your expectations, and he will exceed your expectations. Catch your child doing something right so you can praise him. Tell your child what you would like him to do, and then praise him for doing it right. Seeing the joy on my five-year-old grandson's face when we applauded him for catching a ball, or on my one-year-old granddaughter's face when we applauded her first steps, I know there is nothing more powerful than praise!

Praise has certainly played a big role in my life. I remember a very pivotal moment in my life that changed it for the better. I remember it like it was yesterday, even though it was well over fifty years ago. I was in the fifth grade. My teacher, Mrs. Barnes, praised me for knowing the right answer to a math question, remarking how smart she thought I was because I was the only one in the whole class who knew the answer. Actually, that was the first time that anyone had ever said I was smart, and I was ten years old!

Prior to that, I had attended a Lutheran church school, starting at age five. The whole school was about the choir. Since I could not carry a tune in a bucket (although I came from musical parents), I was ridiculed and given punishment work to do while everyone else was singing in the choir.

Obviously, I did not like that school. I felt ostracized due to my lack of musical ability and was not inspired or motivated in any way. I felt like a failure, and my grades reflected my low opinion of myself. Although I was later tested and found to have an IQ of 149, up to that point, I had always thought of myself as dumb. I remember my mother saying to me in the fourth grade that I was not worth spending private tuition on, pointing out that my grades were quite disappointing. My mother constantly compared me to my brother (who went to the same school), by saying *"Thank God, at least I have one smart kid,"* referring to my brother (who could also sing!) When my mother transferred me to public school in the fifth grade (so as not to waste any more of her hard-earned money on a dumb kid), it was the best thing that could have happened. Since I had already learned some of the math work in church school, I knew the correct answers. When my fifth grade teacher praised me, it made a big difference in my life. Someone actually thought I was smart! I would have done anything to prove her right. It was amazing what a little praise could do! For the first time in my life, I was motivated and went on to prove how right she was by getting all A's after that. My mother couldn't believe it, but my father (who had believed I was smart all along) just applauded me. This is what the spark of praise and positive reinforcement can do. All of a sudden, my self-concept changed—at age ten. Thank God it did! If it hadn't been for a little praise, I might have been lost forever. I so liked the feeling of being praised and being on top that I vowed to stay there! (Thank you, Mrs. Barnes!)

Pay attention to how you treat your children. Are you empowering them or crippling them? Praise empowers them. Criticism cripples them. Keep the desired outcome in mind. What is it that you want to do for your children, whom you say you love so much?

Childhood should be *fun*—a time when kids are allowed to explore themselves and learn about life. The purpose of being a parent should be to raise a joyful child, not one who is always angry. When your child expresses anger, it is a cover-up emotion. Really what your child is feeling is frustration that he has not succeeded in living up to your expectations of him. When a child feels that he cannot live up to the expectations of the most important person in his life, he will be ill-prepared to handle life. Since you are the adult, perhaps you need to change your expectations so they are age-appropriate or suitable for your child. Praise your child when he does live up to your new expectations. Praise inspires better behavior.

Good behavior can only be *inspired* in children. It can't be beaten or punished into them. A child will act according to his own self-image. If you build a child up and make him feel special, that child will act like he is special. If you put a child down and tell him how bad, dumb, or inadequate he is, he will start behaving in accordance with that self image (which is actually programmed into the child by his parents when that child is too young to know any better!). You don't toughen children up by tearing them down. Treat your child like he is special at home, and he will always be special in life!

I grew up knowing that, at the very least, I was loved, no matter what I did. If you're lucky enough to have grown up loved, you're very lucky indeed. Being unconditionally loved gives a child the freedom to be who he is. To be unconditionally loved doesn't mean that the child is perfect or is always *liked*; but *to be loved* is the best gift a parent can give their child. It validates who that child is before he can validate himself. Your love and approval should not be conditional and should never be based just on your child's behavior.

When you spank, punch, or hit a child, you are teaching that child that physical violence is appropriate when a person can't control their anger. Children then get the message that it is okay to hit, kick, or punch siblings or playmates. That is the wrong message to send! Hitting a child to stop him from hitting others is ridiculous! There is even some recent research that has proven that kids who get spanked have IQ's that are five percent lower than kids that don't get spanked, and spanking definitely lowers their self-esteem. Spanking also develops anti-social behavior, sending the message that it's okay for big people to hit little people. Although children would rather be physically abused than mentally abused, think what it is that you are teaching them—that physical violence and assault are okay. While the memory of any physical pain will go away in time, the memory of any mental abuse will stay with your child for a long time and will dramatically affect his future. When you call your child a derogatory name, you are actually throwing darts at your child. Picture your child's beautiful face and then picture yourself throwing darts into his eyes. That is what you are doing when you call your child stupid, lazy, worthless, or bad. Children learn what they live and give back what they get. Is that the kind of behavior you want your children to emulate?

Parents write on the chalkboard of their child's life everyday, and some things are very hard to erase. Ask yourself, *"Do I want my child to fear me or to love me?"* Patterns are set very early in life. A young girl sees herself through her father's eyes. He is the most important person in the world to her. When a father is abusive and puts that young girl down, she thinks that's exactly what she deserves. When that young girl grows up, she will choose men who are just like her father, who will abuse her and put her down. Is that what you want for your daughter? If you abuse your child mentally or physically, that child will most likely turn out to be the same type of parent that you were since you are your child's most powerful role model. Your child will exhibit the same kind of behavior as a parent that he learned from you, which is to be an abusive parent. Is that what you want for your grandchildren? If not, then stop the pattern right now.

A good example of a product of this poor parental pattern is our dog groomer, who became a friend of mine, and sheepishly shared with me that she was beaten every day (and usually for little or no reason) by her veterinarian father, of whom she was deathly afraid. This poor girl turned to animals for comfort because adults abused her. However, as a young woman, she continued to act out the self-image that was programmed into her by her abusive father. She chose abusive partners who beat her or ran around on her. This woman never got that she deserved more because the one person who could have raised her self-esteem when she was growing up put her down and punished her. Think about what that does to a child. Do you want your children to fear and hate you or to admire you and want to be just like you?

Can you see yourself in your children? Imitation is the sincerest form of flattery. Are your children imitating you by doing what you do? What kind of relationship do you have with your children? Do they actually want to be around you because you're fun and caring? Do their eyes light up when you walk into a room? When they were young, did your children follow you everywhere eagerly looking for a sign of affection?

Remember to always talk to your kids about things that don't matter so that they will feel comfortable talking to you about things that do matter when they get older. Please don't make it a chore for your children to be around you. Otherwise, when your children grow up, they will choose not to be around you. Is that what you want? A child will always come back to where he was loved and received the most *petting*, but not to where he received the most put-downs (which just made him feel ashamed of himself).

The best way to control your child is to raise him to have a healthy self-image and to promote the belief that your child is letting both himself and you down if he does not behave in accordance with that self-image. Children should feel good about who they are. Their parents should applaud their achievements, from their first step to their college degree. However, parents should let their children take credit for their accomplishments on their own. When you instill respect in your child for himself and you, his behavior will become something that will make both of you proud. He will then learn to respect your opinion. Remember, respect can only be commanded, not demanded; and it does not come from a child being reprimanded!

The job of a parent is to prepare children for life, not to protect them from life. If you communicate to your children that the world is a scary place, they will grow up afraid of the world. Teach children caution, but don't teach them fear. Teach them instead to believe in themselves and that they are capable of handling any situation that may occur. Fear is only a failure to cope.

Foster independence in your child. The more you do for your child, the more you take away your child's ability to do for himself. Teach your child to like himself, independent of the opinion of others. Then he will not be tempted by peer pressure and give control to others in order to get their approval. Instead, teach your child to make his own decisions and to stand by them.

Don't be an enabler. A dear friend of mine has a twenty-seven-year-old son who doesn't have a car or a job because my friend did everything for him his whole life. My friend was an enabler—a very loving mother, who raised a very dependent son. That was certainly not the result she wanted.

Avoid being a *helicopter parent*, constantly hovering over your kids. Let go and let them grow! There are some parents who won't even let their kids walk a block from the bus stop when they're coming home from school and insist that their children be within their sight at all times. This certainly does not foster independence in their children. On the other hand, I had *free-range* parents, who allowed me to walk many blocks by myself when I was five-and-a-half to catch a streetcar, then to transfer to a bus to get to the church school in downtown Baltimore. I was also allowed to play outside everyday, wherever and with whomever I wanted, as long as I came home for dinner, which I always did. I learned independence at a very early age, and could always stand on my own two feet.

The best thing you can teach a child is *self-sufficiency*. Teach your children to help themselves, but not to help themselves to your money. Parents should not become people to lean on, but should be people who make leaning unnecessary because they teach their children how to stand straight on their own two feet. Actually, if you carry your children too long, their legs become week and won't work anymore. Why would we as parents spend so much time teaching our kids to walk and then want to *carry* them for the rest of their lives? The more you do for a child, the less you are requiring that child to do on his own. That can actually cripple your child and make him irresponsible. It is like tying your child's legs together and expecting him to walk. Parents need to take a *stand* and make their children *stand* on their own two feet. Your job as a parent is to raise an independent, self-sufficient adult who doesn't need a parent when he is grown, but who still wants to be around his parents because he loves them. A child may want to grow up and be just like his parents, but the best parents really just help their child to give birth to *himself!*

Many *baby boomers* are unfortunately raising a generation of *boomerang kids*, who just won't leave their *basement* because everything at home is paid for by the parents. After having funded their children's college education for years, many parents are now being told by their children that they can't find a job that is *worthy* of them. Therefore, the kids do not work; and the parents have to work even harder to keep supporting them. By raising their kids with such a false sense of entitlement, these parents are actually instilling in their children the thought that it's okay to remain kids for the rest of their lives. *Don't make growing up optional!* Don't enable your kids, by emotionally and mentally stifling their ambition and teaching them *entitlement*. Good parents should instill inspiration and motivation in their kids instead of just indulging them, which only leads to inertia and inaction on the kids part.

The problem with most parents is that they love their kids so much that they don't *require* enough of them. These parents want to make life easy for their children—easier than they had it when they were growing up. The problem with this is that they are actually taking away their children's sense of ambition and accomplishment, without even knowing it. When we make life too easy for our children, they become soft and pliable and never learn to be resilient to life's lessons. Is that what we want for our children? Don't take away from your kids the sense of pride that they could get from doing something on their own. Why is it that we as parents want to give our children everything but the sense of achievement that we got from overcoming our challenges and doing things on our own? Allow your kids to grow.

Don't fund their dysfunction. A mother should be a M.O.M. not an A.T.M.! *Lay off your offspring!*

Don't let your children manipulate you and send you on a *guilt trip*. Take a trip to the mall, to the movies, or to Italy instead!

The best parents just really want their children to grow up and be somebody on their own, which means that, in time, your children will leave you. When you get to that point, you can tell yourself that you have succeeded because your fledglings have flown away and do not need you anymore. However, if their nest was warm and happy, the fledglings will always return to visit.

The best way to get your children to go in the right direction is to *lead the way!* Don't lose your own identity when raising your children. If you just live for your children, you will have a problem letting go when those children grow into the strong, independent beings they were meant to be. My kids turned out great because I maintained an independent identity while raising them. I provided a strong role model by setting an example and encouraging the belief that they could be whatever they wanted to be. Actually, I believed in both of my kids long before anyone else did; but I also taught them how to believe in themselves.

Become the kind of parent that your kids would want to emulate— independent, separate, strong, and sensitive. Where your children are concerned, be a *dream booster*, not a *dream buster*. Always believe in your kids, until and even after they become old enough to believe in themselves.

Fortunately, my parents provided a good role model in my life. Unfortunately though, I only had my father in my life for eighteen years. He died at age fifty-two, but he made a big impact on my life while he was around. My fondest memories of him revolve around the joy that he spread. Everybody loved my father and wanted to be around him because he was so loving and so much fun. Some of my earliest memories were about chasing my little friends off my father's lap so I could sit there; after all, he was *my* father! My father played the guitar and sang and basically always had a great time in his short life. I always wanted to be as carefree and happy as my father when I grew up, but fate determined that I would have to take more responsibility to make a living. Since my father was a salesman and chose to play harder than he worked, it was always feast-or-famine in our family. My mother was the only one who got a paycheck every Friday. I remember that my brother, Dad, and I would meet her for lunch, cash her check, and then dine royally at a restaurant. My parents always drank Manhattans on Fridays, and my brother and I were given the cherries to savor (even though they had a tinge of alcohol in them). To this day, I love Manhattans, as I always associate them with Fridays, payday, and celebrating good times! By Monday, though, my parents were broke. I remember my mother would have to borrow a dollar from my aunt to buy ground beef to make dinner for the rest of the week. Although we were always short on funds, we sure had fun! I always knew my family was poor, but it didn't really matter. I grew up house-poor but family-rich!

My father had many other good points (although being a provider was not one of them). I don't really know how my father did it; but if I did, I could patent it and make a fortune! My father could control me with the expressions on his face. When I was growing up, I remember I would rather do anything than to see a look of disappointment on my father's face if I should let him down in some way. My father never raised his voice in anger, but the *look on his face* told me that he expected more of me because he held me in such high regard. I became an overachiever because of my *father's face* and, after the fifth grade, wouldn't dare bring home a B when I knew my father thought I should get all As. Actually, I was so busy living up to my father's good opinion of me that I didn't have time to get into trouble. My Dad always let me know that I was supposed to live up to the mental pictures he had of me. After all, I was *Daddy's girl!*

Although my father died when I was eighteen, he had a lot of influence in my life. One of the things I remember most about my father besides the *look* is that he always took the time to play with us as kids. My father was a salesman, with a salesman's outgoing personality, who just loved to have fun. He taught us that fun was actually important and worthwhile. (Thanks, Dad!)

Since my father worked strictly on commission, he never made much money, especially since he would rather be home playing with us. Sometimes our family didn't know where our next meal was coming from, but my brother and I didn't really know we were poor. We were so *rich in love* that neither of us felt deprived. If I had a choice to grow up in a household rich in love or rich in material things, I would choose rich in love!

Anyone who grows up *rich in love* will make his own way in life and be able to create whatever he needs. Love is the most important thing in a child's life, and the most important gift that a parent can give a child. I don't mean *smothering* love. I mean *supportive* love. There's a difference between *mothering love* and *smothering love*. You can never give a child too much love if it helps to foster his independence and supports him in being who he wants to be. If you want to give your children *everything*, just give them love. *Love is everything!*

Yet how many parents spend the bulk of their time providing materialistic things for their children like TVs, cell phones, video games, and all kinds of gadgets and toys but never give their children what they really need, which is the parent's time and unconditional love? Parents shouldn't hover over their kids. Instead they should let their children know that they just want to be with them because they enjoy them as human beings. That way both can enjoy a relaxed respect for each other.

Spend your time with your children *creating* instead of *criticizing*. Finding fault doesn't fix anything. Do not hold your kids responsible for things they can't control. Don't miss all the good things that your children do and see only the bad. Celebrate your child's individual progress and successes without comparing him to anyone other than who he was yesterday. The best thing you can teach a child is to love himself. You do that by first loving him unconditionally, no matter what! Children learn what they live, but you have to talk to them before their ears close!

Creative play is very important in a child's life. When I was a child, my brother and I were lucky if we could afford a ball; but we played outside in all kinds of weather, using our imaginations to make up a myriad of games. Not only were there the normal games like hide and seek, jump rope, and hopscotch; but we also picked mulberries and created a whole winery on the open lot behind us.

Barrels, boards, and plastic chutes functioned as a distillery, where we squashed mulberries, fermented them in barrels, and bottled them in coke bottles. We spent hours in productive play, not just mindlessly or vicariously living through a TV. We made go-carts from scraps of materials. Borrowing a few blankets from inside our house to be used as tents, we transformed our back yard into a carnival with a fortune teller, a wheel of fortune, clowns, and a game of ring toss on coke bottles. When we were kids, we used our imaginations and whatever else we could find that was free; but we always had lots of fun. Our parents had to beg us to come in to eat—we were that excited about our play! I had a very happy childhood because I was allowed to play a lot, any way I wanted; and that play became very creative and constructive.

My brother and I also did anything we could to make money—returning coke bottles for two cents, finding and selling golf balls back to golfers, and charging admission (two cents) to get into our circus tent. In those days, it cost five cents to go to the movies; and we were able to go to the matinee every Saturday with the money we made. Boy, were we proud of ourselves! We weren't given anything but the opportunity to let our imaginations run wild!

Kids nowadays live much more structured lives, where every game is provided for them; and most games are sedentary. Children are rushed from planned activity to planned activity and are not given any time for creative play or to use their own imaginations. Unstructured play is extremely important for a child. Parents would be amazed at what children could create on their own if given the opportunity and the time. Give your children the chance to *explore themselves*, for therein lies the key to their future.

Encourage *whimsy* and *wonder* in your kids. Excite and explore your children's imaginations; for somewhere in their imaginations, they are creating themselves. Imagination is actually more powerful than knowledge, for it is the beginning of the creative process. Make teaching your children how to use their imaginations part of their education.

Even as an adult, it is important for us to nurture our inner child as we take time out to play. Play refreshes us and restores inner joy.

Take the time to play not only with your child, but also with your inner child. Make each day a magical, fun kind of day and let your inner child out to play!

I love playing with my young grandchildren because they bring out the youngest part of me, which is buried deep inside. We make up games and just create fun. I gave my granddaughter a puppet theatre and hand puppets for Christmas one year when she was two and a half. Creative play allows a child to make up her own stories, which she loved doing. My granddaughter, Katy, was always the good girl in her stories (which matched her self-concept), and *Nathan* was the bad boy, whom she had to teach a lesson. It is amazing what happens when you stimulate your children's imaginations. Grandparents, who have more time, are usually good at this. By emphasizing your children's roots and letting them bond with extended family, you insure that your child will always feel connected to the base where he was born—his source. A child should be proud of his roots, which connect him. Those roots will make him always want to return home—at least for a little while. These roots are what your child will pass on to his children. Your family should be like a tree, where the branches grow in different directions; but the roots always remain as one—thereby ensuring that each member of the family will always be a part of the other!

Families are tied together by their roots. The best things you can give your children in life are *roots and wings*. *Wings* so that they can fly on their own, and *roots* so that they will always remember where they came from and want to return to their source.

Once your children are ready, you must teach them how to fly so they can soar in search of themselves. When your children feel they are ready to fly, never hold them back. You can be the *wind beneath their wings*, but let your children test their own wings. Just be their safe place to fall. If they do fall, kiss their wounds, and encourage them to try again until they can soar on their own.

Teach your children to love you, but not to need you. The goal in raising children should be to teach your child to be independent. Someone said that raising children should be like shooting a bow and arrow, where you just point a child in the right direction and let go. Hopefully, the children will reach their target—independence. When we teach our children that they must stick with us to survive, it is damaging to our children. We want them to thrive, not just to survive.

A parent's role is not to be a policeman, nor should we ever instill fear in our children by threatening them. To say to a child, *"I am going to put you in jail, give you away to the bogeyman, put you up for adoption, or just get rid of you"* erodes any sense of security that a child may have. Also a mother should not say to a child, *"Just wait until your father gets home!"* implying that the child is going to get punished, scolded, or beaten when the father returns. This makes the child dread his father's coming home. It also puts the father in the position of having to immediately correct the child (whom he hasn't seen all day), when all he really wants to do is be with that child and hug him. A mother should handle each situation as it occurs during the day and correct improper behavior herself. She will earn more respect from her child if she is an authority figure and doesn't pawn all the discipline off on the father. The role of a father is to be a provider, teacher, leader, and protector; but he should also be there for his kids to know and love as a human being with a warm heart and a soft spot for them. Mothers should be *mothers* and not *martyrs*. Actually, the best thing a mother can give her child is a happy and fulfilled mom.

Many mothers nowadays are working outside of the home. That should make those mothers relish all the more the time spent with their children when they do get home. It is certainly important for a child to get to spend quality time with each parent, who is hopefully not caught up in their own chores or TV when they do get home. Dinnertime is a great time for each family member to share the day's experiences. It is not the time to live vicariously in front of the TV. Instead of turning on the TV and turning off your child, encourage sharing and creative play that you can participate in as a family. Give your kids materials and let them make up games. Exercise their imagination and their fantasies, for therein lies their future. Convert your child's Xbox into an *in-box*, where he can create fantasies on his own. In an era when most homes have more TVs than they have people living in them, please don't let TV stifle your child's creativity.

In fact, don't let TV stifle your own dreams, either, by distracting you from thinking about them. One cannot be creative and be passively entertained at the same time. Tell yourself, *Maybe it's time to turn off the TV and to just discover me!* When the TV is on, your creativity is off. Which pastime do you think would yield better results?

Many of today's children, whose families are the richest monetarily, are deprived of the time to create. Remember, nothing bad ever comes from inside of our children, unless it is put there externally. Why do we, as parents, let external influences teaching violence and fierce competition exploit our children; and why do we, as parents, allow our children to be exposed to predators and pornography on the Internet? Is it because we are too lazy or too busy to teach our children how to explore themselves? Some parents would rather use the TV and the Internet as babysitters, forgetting that their most important role in life is to be a role model to their children. As parents, we propagated them. Now our role is to play with them, pray with them, and most of all praise them, thereby keeping them from becoming prey for predators (who have more time for our children than we do!). There is nothing material that you can give a child that could make up for a lack of maternal or paternal companionship.

A recent poll determined that the thing a child wants most is to spend more time with his parents and to know that his parents are interested in him. Family time is a jewel that your children inherit and will want to pass on to their children. The family jewels that children inherit are priceless moments of family fun, which are forever etched in a child's memory. Those jewels totally affect who and what your children will become and who your grandchildren will be.

So many rich kids grow up really poor because their parents are so busy staying rich that they don't have time for their children. These parents give their children's care over to full-time nannies. Then, in order to pay for the nanny's upkeep, as well as their own, these parents have to spend even more hours away from the home. Their children are being raised by surrogates.

If a nanny assists with household chores, shopping, laundry, and cooking so that the parents can spend more quality time with their children, then that is a plus; but parents should never let a nanny replace them in the lives of their children. After all, they are your children; and there is nothing more important than your spending quality time with them while they are young.

If you want to know how good a parent you have been, ask yourself, *"Do my kids show interest every time I walk into the room? Do they gravitate toward me or avoid me? Do they take me for granted or ignore me?"* Don't let another day go by before you become the kind of parent your kids would adore. This is the most important role you will ever play in your life. Play it well. The rewards are astonishing.

Most important of all, don't be a *revolving door* parent, who is in and out of your child's life as the mood suits you. Be there constantly and consistently for your children. *No parent wants to have a love child who sends him hate mail!*

Children are not disposable! They are in your lives forever once you have chosen to conceive them. To disown them, ignore them, or pretend that they don't exist because they have disappointed you in some way is like disowning a part of your body. If you injure your finger in an accident, you cannot pretend it is no longer your finger just because it hurts. You must do whatever you have to do to help your finger to heal, or it will get worse. Once your finger has healed, it will be part of your whole again, just as your children will always be part of you if you love them in spite of whatever they may do.

Sometimes, parents may not get along with each other; but it is important to remember to never argue with your spouse in front of your children. Don't give your kids a front row seat to your squabbles! Yelling obscene and angry words at your spouse in front of your children actually scares them. After you and your spouse have said nasty things to each other, you may kiss and make up; but your kids won't forget. When parents argue in front of their kids, it shakes their kids to the core since their parents are the only security these children have. No child ever wants to see his parents break up, but even less does that child want to witness his parents constant bickering and name calling. For your family to become known as *"the Bickersons"* could be very detrimental to your children.

Couples who say they are staying together *for the kids* and then constantly argue in front of their kids are not doing their kids any favors. Just think about what kind of a role model for a relationship these couples are providing. What will their children's mental picture of a marriage be? If you can't live in harmony in front of your children with the person you are supposed to love for the rest of your life, then maybe you need to separate. Remember, kids would rather come from a broken home than to live in one!

Take the temperature of your home on a daily basis. Is it warm and healthy, or is it overheated and ready to explode at any moment? If mutual respect exists between two parents; but every now and then disagreements do erupt, those disagreements should be held in private and kept private. Sometimes when a parent becomes angry, he may think that it is necessary to talk about what is on his mind at the moment that is making him so unhappy; but that parent should never bring up the past or unrelated instances that have occurred. The object of an argument should be to be heard and not to win; but most importantly, those arguments should not be within earshot of your children. Why would you want to win an argument, anyway, if it makes your partner a loser?

The thing that is most important in an argument is how you end the fight. At least allow your partner to retain his or her dignity. Ask yourself, *"What can I do today to enhance my partner's happiness, relish our relationship, and keep our family functional?"* Don't be a fault-finder or a scorekeeper. Instead learn to value peace, harmony, and your family's happiness above all. Before beginning an argument, always be clear in your mind what you want the outcome to be (which should really just be a better understanding of each other's perspectives).

Kids grow up differently in a home where they can detect affection and love between their parents. Isn't that really what you want to model for your children? Don't they deserve to learn about love and emotion from two parents who can demonstrate it openly in front of them? If you can't fight fair or find fulfillment with your partner, then it might be better to live apart, instead of cheating on your partner or running each other ragged with disagreements. If you can't agree not to disagree in front of your children, perhaps you should seek professional counseling or separate quarters. Even worse than constant arguing though, is when apathy sets in; and the two parents ignore each other. When children live in an emotionally barren environment, where there is no affection between their parents, there is no role model for them to follow in their future relationships. These children then become emotionally handicapped. Sometimes partners do much better apart and become much better parents when they're not living together. Separately, each parent may be able to spend quality time alone with the children avoiding the constant bickering that took so much of the parents' time when they were together.

Don't ever use your children as pawns or weapons against your spouse. Children should always be allowed to love both parents equally. Never sabotage your child's relationship with the other parent or make that child feel guilty for loving the other parent. Believe me, I know how difficult that can be—especially if you're angry at your spouse for having wronged you! However, the other parent is still part of your child's heart. The relationship your child has with each of his parents should be up to your child and that parent. If one parent deliberately goes away and chooses not to be in their child's life, let the child judge that parent for himself. Never transfer your hurt feelings about your partner on to your child or use your child to gain information about the other parent.

Don't expect your kids to think or act like adults or to understand adult issues between their parents. Keep your issues out of your child's life. Let your child form his own opinion about each of his parents. If you put the other parent down too much, your child may actually end up hating you. Remember that the other parent is part of your child too, and your child needs to learn for himself what each parent is about. Having a healthy relationship with both parents is important to a child because it will determine how healthy a relationship that child will have with himself and others in the future.

Never try to alienate a child from the other parent. For one thing, you could lose custody of your child if parental alienation were to be proven in court. For another, it could cause that child to turn against you. Hopefully, you can at least be friends with your ex while you share the responsibility for raising your kids. If not (especially when one parent refuses to be a parent), let the kids find out for themselves. After many episodes of being let down by an uncaring, absentee parent, a child will actually alienate himself from that parent so he will not be hurt anymore. When that occurs, your child will eventually accept the reality that he has one uncaring parent and will not be angry with the one who does care. Just always be there to support your child yourself. Let him know that he is loved by at least one responsible adult.

It is natural for a child to want his parents to get along. Frequently, a child will actually blame himself when his parents are getting a divorce. I remember that at one time, my son thought that he had caused his dad to go away because he got a D on a spelling test in the first grade. He was usually an A or B student and really thought that his getting a D made his dad leave. My son even tried to punish himself, thinking that it was his fault that his father left. It took a lot to finally convince my son otherwise.

When my children were growing up, I was a single mom for seven years. Their father chose not to consistently be a part of their lives when he moved to a different state. That really wreaked havoc in my mind, because, in my world, daddies just didn't voluntarily go away. I had to be both mother and father to my kids, breadwinner and nurturer; but they were always the most important thing in my life. Even though I had to work a lot of hours, I always made the time to be there for my kids—for homework, school activities, and games; and we took lots of family vacations together. Thank God, I also had my mother, who could be there when I wasn't. It broke my heart that my kids were hurt by their departing dad, but I did everything I could to make up for him. I always taught my children that they were loveable, even though their dad had deserted them; and I made it a point to never put my kids down. I also taught them that they could do or be whatever they wanted if they just believed in themselves. Eventually, my kids gave up the hope for and a belief in a *fantasy father*.

Later on, a new father (my current husband) came into their lives as an exemplary male role model and taught my children that there's a difference between a *father* and a *Dad!* My husband actually earned the title *Dad* by consistently being there for my children, by loving them, supporting them, and performing all the *Dad duties*, which for him were a labor of love. My children and my husband are not connected by *blood*, but they are certainly connected by *heart*. To this day, my kids adore this *Dad*, and no longer talk to their former father (their choice!) My daughter even asked my husband (her *new Dad*) to give her away when she got married. My husband has never put my children down and left the discipline (which there wasn't much of) to me. To say that my children didn't need discipline was probably not true. I just always thought that they needed inspiration more, and my emphasis was always on inspiring good behavior instead of dwelling on bad behavior. My children have never let me down. Perhaps God thought I deserved good kids because of what I had gone through, or perhaps I just created them. Anyway, I can't tell you how proud I am of my children and also of the parents they have become!

One of the things I initiated when my kids were teenagers was to start *Family Feast*—a gourmet dining night, once a week, just for the four of us. There were two teams—the females (my daughter and I) were pitted against the males (my husband and son). Each team was responsible for cooking gourmet delights from favorite recipes. The females were responsible for cooking appetizers and soups or salads, while the males would make the entrée and dessert. The next week we would switch courses, and one team would try to outdo the other. These evenings provided a lot of camaraderie, some friendly competition, and yielded some delicious delicacies. A fun time was had by all. My kids, my husband, and I really looked forward to these Family Feasts. Consequently, my daughter decided she wanted to be a chef and actually went to culinary college. Although she has chosen another career (which she has excelled at), to this day, she is an excellent cook (her lucky husband!). My son can also cook (even though he won't admit it to his wife!). The sharing and caring were priceless, and I tried to foster other such experiences that featured family time.

Actually, I couldn't have designed my children to be any more successful, caring, or awesome adults than they are. Think of how you would like your children to turn out and then program them positively with that end in mind. The thing your children need from you the most is not your bank account, but your acceptance and your approval.

Don't withhold it! Why wait another minute to tell your children how wonderful they are and how important they are to you?

I always taught my children that the most important thing in life was to *believe in yourself.* I also taught them that a person can't be an *under-believer* and an *overachiever.* Nor can someone be an *over-believer* and an *underachiever!* My children were raised with the concept that if they could *conceive it and believe it, they could achieve it.*

As a result, my children have turned out to be very successful independent adults. My son, as the hard-working head of The Creig Northrop Team, has just been recognized as the number one real estate team nationally for all companies in America!

There was a time when my son worked for me when I founded *The Northrop Team* which also became the No. 1 team in Long and Foster Real Estate. I remember making the remark during my speeches that if I ever got beaten by anyone in real estate sales, "*Lord let it be my son!*" (From my lips to God's ears!) I used to tell my son that if he could ever beat me in sales, I would come to work for him. I guess I created that too! My son subsequently founded his own team, The Creig Northrop Team, and decided to compete against me to establish his own name in real estate. I did not want to compete with my son; and so the year that he beat me, I came to work for him as part of his team. My son has taken his business to a whole new level. *I had a dream,* which I accomplished; but my son's dreams are so much greater than mine that he has accomplished so much more. I have no doubt that his beliefs will take him wherever he wants to go. My daughter, Nicole, on the other hand, started in a completely different business in another state, and her beliefs have taken her to the top of her field also. Nicole, who lives in Dallas, is a very successful senior sales manager with The Four Seasons, one of the top national hotel chains. Both my son and daughter are happily married to the perfect partners for them.

I'm now in the process of teaching my grandchildren *creationalism.* When they're in the car with me, I marvel at how many parking places right up front that the older ones can create. When they were young teenagers, both of them loved taking credit for doing this, as well as *creating* tables in crowded restaurants. I'm also teaching my younger grandchildren creative play, but most of all just to believe in themselves.

One of the greatest rewards in my life is to see how well my children have turned out and what great parents they have become. When I think of my family, I know I must have done something right, based on results! The two most important things I have ever given my children were unconditional love and a belief that they were special—and they are!

As you think back about your own childhood, ask yourself, "*Did I become the adult that I always wanted to be when I was a child—you know, the one who was always understanding and so much fun to be around?*" If not, it's never too late to make an impact on some child's life as well as to change your own. Just think— one word of praise could make all the difference in the world in the life of a child!

If you want to be a great parent........

Put on your _partici_-pants, and teach your children the

fun-damentals of life!

When families are connected heart-to-heart,

time and distance can't keep them apart!

8

Facing Your Fears

Just what is fear, anyway, and what is there really to fear in life?

Fear implies a lack of belief in ourself that we will be able to handle whatever challenges we are given. Since we are overcoming challenges every day, the only real fear is the *fear of the unknown*. When the unknown becomes known, it is no longer scary because it can be dealt with. The *monsters* that we fear live in the depth of our imaginations, but only in the dark. Turn on the lights, and monsters disappear because they were never real anyway.

My favorite definition of fear is <u>F</u>alse <u>E</u>vidence <u>A</u>ppearing <u>R</u>eal, where the first letter of each word spells *fear*. Fear is not really based on fact. Fear stems from our beliefs, which actually get their basis from our fabrications or fantasies. The truth is that most of us actually fabricate fear in our minds by playing the *"what if"* game.

"What if" the worst happened? What would we do? That *"what if"* may never happen; but even if it did, why do we not have enough faith in ourselves to believe that we could handle any situation that may occur? After all, we have proven time and again that disasters can be dealt with and dissolved. However, instead of proceeding confidently in life with that belief in mind, most of us choose to worry about things that never happen. That must mean that *worry works* since

most of the things we worry about don't ever happen. Worry, then, is like garlic or a silver cross that is used to ward off vampires. The only problem is that worry actually becomes the vampire by sucking our blood, which is the precious time that we spend worrying, when that same time could be better spent in joy and happiness.

Worry actually implies a lack of belief in our ability to handle whatever may come along. Why can't we recognize that we are competent and are actually capable of coping with any calamity? Why create calamites, though, when we could be creating calm? Worry actually sets negative thoughts in motion, and entices our self-conscious into believing those negative thoughts into reality. Since our thoughts are so powerful, they are capable of making a situation materialize that we worried about but never really wanted to have happen in the first place. Actually, the more constantly and passionately that we worry about something, the quicker that thing will manifest itself. Since the self-conscious doesn't know the difference between reality and an abnormality, it creates what it thinks we want. In essence, then, we end up creating what we fear but didn't really want to have happen. Why create what you don't want? Why think about a thing at all if it's something that you really don't want to have happen? Remember, *what you think about repeatedly replicates itself.*

Instead of being a *worrier*, think of yourself as a *warrior*, confident that you can conquer any situation or tame any terror that may occur. A *worrier* propels fear into reality. A *warrior* takes action, which is the enemy of fear. A *warrior* actually terminates fear dispelling it before it can do any harm. For example, let's take a crisis situation: pretend you're in a room with eleven hungry tigers ready to pounce on you because they perceive you as their dinner. What would you do? Would you run, scream, pray, or have a heart attack? Well, you could just... *stop pretending!* Remember, I said *pretend.* Isn't that what fears are anyway, just *pretend?* Stop pretending and your fears will fade away. Fears are just *paper tigers.* Crumple them up and throw them away!

Actually there are really only two things that might be fearful in life—the fear of being devoured or of not having enough to devour.

If you can say "*I ate today, and I was not eaten!*", what else is there to fear?

Fear makes you worry about just *surviving* instead of thinking of *thriving*. In order to just *survive*, you throw away every chance to *thrive*. When you think about *thriving*, you are creating happiness and abundance. Fear connected with anything other than survival is useless and makes mountains out of molehills. When you focus on just surviving, you are operating from a basis of fear, implying a desire to keep away from hunger or harm in an "*I ate and I was not eaten*" mode. What would you rather focus on—surviving or thriving? Remember, whatever you focus on manifests itself! When you become a warrior instead of a worrier, you block out fear. A warrior is afraid of nothing, regards everything as a challenge, and looks for ways to win at that challenge. Start by asking yourself, "*What is it that I am afraid of?*" Trust your *warrior within* to cope with any calamity. Just don't create calamities. Instead of *fabricating fears, instill inspiration* both in yourself and others to create joy and abundance in life.

Every day, we must choose whether to face the future with *apprehension or anticipation*. Wouldn't it be wonderful if we could face each day with the same anticipation and wonder as a child on Christmas morning? Given a choice, why would anyone choose to wake up fearing or dreading each day? Actually, the fear or apprehension about any situation can be worse than the reality of that situation. Don't let yourself be paralyzed by fear. Fear stays with you. Fear creates indecision, which creates inaction. Only action can initiate and create positive results. Are you excited but afraid at the same time when you face a new challenge? Flex your mental muscles to summon up the courage that will free you from the futility of fear.

Form a strong inner ally with yourself. Spend your time thinking about what matters most to you and the positive things you would like to have in your life. Believe in your ability to create those things and the universe will support your effort. Tell yourself, "*Even if I fail, I will stand by me anyway!*", because in reality you are your own best friend. Change can become a creative challenge when the fear of failure is removed.

One of the most frightening things that ever happened to me was totally unexpected and unbelievably scary. I know I did not create it because I could not have even conceived of it before it happened, but it happened for some reason.

This event could have crippled me mentally and would have been a real setback to my career if I had let it make a difference in my life.

It all started one bright, sunny Sunday afternoon, while I was showing a house in my old neighborhood. Suddenly, I was attacked and raped by a potential buyer, who completely took me by surprise. After doing everything according to real estate code—meeting the prospect at my office and having him follow me in his car—I was attacked in one of my own listings, in my own neighborhood, in broad daylight! In those days, agents didn't usually pre-qualify a prospect before showing a home, but I had asked this man a lot of questions about himself and his family and was satisfied with the answers. This prospect was a well-dressed blonde man of average height and build, and I never suspected a thing until he pulled a knife on me in the second story bedroom of the home I was showing.

Needless to say, I was shocked and scared to death! The sellers were not home, and a neighbor next door was mowing his lawn, so I knew no one would hear me if I screamed. The rapist had brought a black bag in with him, (which I thought contained a camera), but in reality held a knife and some duct tape. All of a sudden, I was in a position of having to negotiate for my life, and I was scared to death. This was the most important negotiation I had ever been in, and the man with the weapon definitely had the upper hand! I just wanted to survive—so I did what I do best, I negotiated and tried to reason with the rapist. I did whatever I had to do to stay alive!

In the end, he did leave me alive to tell this story, after hitting me several times to shut me up. (I guess I was ruining his fantasy by pleading for my life!) This experience definitely impacted me and made me realize how precious life is. All I wanted to do was to live through this experience and be able to see my children and my husband again! When the man left, and I realized I was still alive; I was overcome with relief! Tears of joy just streamed down my face even though I was horrified by the thought of what I had just been through and what the outcome could have been! The experience was definitely a catastrophe, but one that I had survived. I realized that after living through such a crisis, I could overcome almost anything in life. The event had scared me, but it hadn't conquered me. It had certainly impacted me, but not enough for me to give up selling real estate!

After the rape, I went back to work in less than a week. The rapist could have killed me, but he could not change me or keep me from doing something I loved. If I had let that person change me because of *fear*, he might as well have killed me. In essence, he would have *killed* who I was. Instead, I continued to be me, which was all I knew how to be.

Although the police never caught the rapist, I refused to stay his victim. I took my power back after the rape, knowing that I had always been a strong person inside and had just become even stronger. Sometimes, *your greatest trial can become your greatest triumph!* I realized that it is really what you *overcome* in life that determines who you *become*.

I thought my worst ordeal was over because I refused to dwell on it in my mind. However, two years later, that same rapist called me to say that he knew where I lived and that he was going to do it again! When my face went white, as if I had seen a ghost, my husband got on the other line; but the man hung up. Since there was no caller ID in those days, my husband dialed *69 repeatedly, but it didn't go through. We reported the call to the police, and then I put it out of my mind and went back to business as usual. I was not going to let fear control me!

People cannot prevent what they cannot predict. However, when fear controls someone's actions, that person is actually running away from life rather than living it. Ask yourself, *"What is it that I am afraid of, and what is the likelihood of that ever happening?"* Don't dwell on your fear, or you may actually create it into reality. Fears that you focus on fester and swell until they become bigger than life.

A nightmare goes away when you open your eyes and wake up. The word *nightmare* comes from the Middle English *nitz* (night) and *mare* (goblin). It refers to a night ride—a flight of fantasy. If you're riding a *goblin*, nothing good can come of it. That's why the word nightmare has its present day connotation. Goblins are not real and exist only in the dark. Open your eyes and they are gone. Don't live your nightmare by going through life with your eyes closed. Change your thoughts by opening your eyes and change your nightmares into dreams, which are something you consciously create while you are awake.

Since you can control your conscious mind and what thoughts you put there, you can create your life the way you want it to be. Do not dwell on your fears. *What you resist persists.* Don't let your fears win. Have faith in yourself that you can handle the worst *what if* in your life, but don't block today's sunshine by worrying about things that may never happen.

The worst thing that ever happened to me in my life (the rape) was something I could not even imagine so I don't think I created it. What I did create was staying alive, putting the incident behind me, and continuing to be *me*. The worst thing that I could have possibly imagined (my husband running off with a friend) had already happened, and it turned out to be the best thing that could have ever happened to me. Although I did not consciously create that event either, I created the result, which was to start a new career, raise a *fenomenal* family on my own, and find the love of my life. When the worse thing you can ever imagine happening in your life has already happened, what else is there to fear? Neither experience crippled me. Both challenges made me a better, stronger person, and now I never face the future with fear. Again, *It is what you overcome in life that determines who you become!*

Don't let your fears stop you from designing your destiny. *Fears don't just keep you from possible failure; they can keep you from future fulfillment!* There is only one thing that makes a dream impossible to achieve, and that is when the fear of failure won't even let you try!

Almost is one of the saddest words in the English language. Sometimes in life, we regret the things we didn't do more than the things we did. If your fears are holding you back, remember that *regret* will eventually replace those fears. Don't let your fears hold you back. An opportunity lost can never be regained!

There is a poignant story entitled *Jason in the Box*, which I will use to illustrate this point. Jason was a cartoon character who looked at lot like *Ziggy*. Unfortunately, Jason had spent most of his adult life curled up in a box that he sincerely wished he could get out of. Jason kept thinking about what *life outside the box* would be like. Finally one day, when Jason's desires became stronger than his fears, he took a deep breath. With all the strength he had in his body, Jason simultaneously pushed his arms and legs against the sides of the box. The box was no match for Jason's desire; and pretty soon, the sides of the box just fell down. Jason was then free to go in any direction he wanted.

Jason, however, was cautious, being unused to his newfound freedom. Although he wanted desperately to leave the box, when Jason looked to the right, he saw a busy street with a lot of cars that he feared might run over him. Because of this fear, Jason hurriedly pulled up the right side of the box. Looking to the left, Jason saw some wild animals, who he feared might devour him, so he pulled the left side of the box up. Straight ahead was a steep cliff. Jason thought, *If I go in that direction, I could fall off that cliff and die.* Quickly, Jason pulled up the front of the box. To the rear, Jason sensed an angry gang of bandits. Fearing that he might be robbed or murdered, Jason pulled up the back of the box. Then Jason noticed a storm brewing up above. Fearing that he would get wet and die from pneumonia, Jason pulled down the top of the box. Now Jason was right back where he had started—bound by the box—and being totally controlled by his fears, which had curtailed his newfound freedom. None of his fears may have ever materialized if Jason had only trusted in his own ability to handle the situation. Unfortunately though, Jason didn't believe in himself enough to do that.

The question then becomes, *Was Jason in the box or was the box in Jason?* Jason chose to react rather than to act. His reactions crippled him, whereas his actions could have brought him freedom and happiness.

Are you smarter than Jason? Are you in control of your own life? Are you in a box, or is there a box inside of you? If so, listen to the sound of your spirit as it keeps banging on the walls of that box, saying, *"Let me out of here!"*

Since your choices to act or react have been programmed in you from the inside, only you can make the choice to change. Change doesn't happen in the middle. It happens only at the edge. When you walk to the edge of the light and are starting to step off into the darkness, you have to believe one of two things—that there will be someone there to catch you if you fall, or that you can fly. In order to step from the known into the unknown, you must be willing to make changes; and change involves risk. In order to move forward, you have to decide that your desires and dreams are greater than your fears. When you replace doubt with desire, guts will get you there! Be willing to take the leap, and make it a leap of faith. In order to fly, you have to let go of the Earth and believe that you can levitate. Actually, there's a little bit of Peter Pan in all of us when we learn to switch on our spiritual electricity and let our spirits soar.

Why is it then that more of us don't fly? Sometime the fear of failure won't even let us try. The only sure way to fail is to not to even try! *You can't fall off the floor!* If your fear of falling keeps you on the floor, that's where you'll stay for the rest of your life. Fortunately, babies don't think that way, or we would all still be crawling! Babies aren't smart enough to know about fear, but they sure know about desire. Desire comes from inside, but fear has to be programmed. Unfortunately, fear has been programmed into many adults who have chosen to stay on the floor because they think it is safer than to try to reach for the ceiling. Not to even make an attempt at something is the best way I know of to ensure certain failure.

What is it that you regret not having done in your life? Is there something that you always wanted to do, from which your fears and insecurities have held you back? Reverse those regrets before it is too late. Don't let your fear of failure hold you back from anything you want to do, because then fear wins over desire. Why do so many people create a *fear factory* in their minds which manufactures fears that block their fantasies? Get rid of the fear factor!

When did fear become such a factor in our lives anyway?

Thank God, we didn't think that way as children. We failed many times (although we don't remember) when learning to walk, ride a bicycle, or catch a ball. Thank God, we didn't give up in fear at our first failures in infancy, or we'd all still be in our cribs! Actually, we didn't know what we couldn't do at a young age. It was our belief that we could succeed at anything that taught us to master everything we can now do in life—but only after many failures. Fortunately, we didn't accept failure as final when we were a child. Then why do we accept failure as final as an adult?

History is filled with incredible accomplishments of people who didn't give up and were actually foolish enough to believe that they could succeed *against all odds!*

When you view failure as taking you one step closer to success; then with each step, if you fall, you will find out what doesn't work. *If you fall eight times, get up nine times!* Keep trying until you find out what does work. If you should happen to fall, try to fall on your back; because if you can look up, you can get up. Remember, no one ever saw a sunset or a rainbow by looking down! Fear is not a natural state. It is learned behavior. Most fears are programmed into us by our parents and are based on their own fears.

What you fear, you create. Just the thought of something that you fear can make that fear materialize. I am the president of our community association, and remember that at one of our general meetings, a neighbor raised her hand and shared how fearful she was of break-ins in our neighborhood. This neighbor said that before going on a recent trip, she had a premonition that someone might break into her home while she was away. Because she was constantly worrying about a break-in and robbery, she even went so far as to leave an envelope with four hundred dollars in cash lying on the counter so that if someone should break in, the intruder would take the cash and leave her other treasures alone. Sure enough, this lady's house did get broken into while she was away; and the thief stole not only the envelope, but other valuables as well. Ironically, this lady's house was the only house in our neighborhood that had ever been broken into! I suggested to her that perhaps her thoughts had created this occurrence, but I don't think she understood what I was saying. She wanted our Board to take action to provide more security in our neighborhood. Unfortunately, I couldn't get thorough to this woman that, although she was not the perpetrator of the break-in, she was certainly the creator! Thoughts are powerful— even negative thoughts. Be careful about what you are programming into reality in your mind. *You just may get it!*

Don't let your fears control you. Don't walk around with permanent PMS, or <u>P</u>oor <u>M</u>e <u>S</u>yndrome, and let it keep you from having what you want. I guarantee you that if it takes a hundred attempts to create something, you will forget 99 of them and only remember the one that succeeded. The secret is not to give up *until you succeed.*

Try something new that you've always wanted to do. When you add some *umph* to the word *try*, you will *triumph*! You can even make your greatest trial into your greatest triumph. Very often, just allowing your beliefs to shine through the darkness can be the greatest challenge. When you light a candle in the sun, no one will see its light; but light that same candle in the dark, and everyone sees its light!

Take control of your own life, but realize that with that control comes responsibility. The responsibility is to keep trying *until you succeed.* Edison invented hundreds of ways that a light bulb would not light until he invented the one way that it would. View failure as a fertilizer that will nurture the seeds of your success. If you're frightened by life, you will run from your opportunities. Instead, learn to trust in yourself and believe that you will succeed. *Self-trust* is the best trust fund you can build, and the only way to get *rich rewards.* Remember, *every great oak was once just a nut that just stood its ground!*

Experience is the best teacher, but experience is not what you get from a college degree or a paid job. Experience is what you learn about life by living it. Know that it is not really what happens to you that matters. It is how you choose to handle what happens to you that makes all the difference in how your life turns out. Experience does not come from what happens to you. It comes from what you choose to do about what happens to you. You can sit around all day and say, "Woe is me!", or you can say, "Whoa, what am I doing to me?"

Don't be an excuse expert. Use the same time it would take to fabricate an excuse about why you couldn't do something to honestly examine your role in why you did not get the results you wanted. Only then can you make changes and build a firm foundation for a more fruitful future—one that is not based on fear or regret.

Paralyze resistance with persistence. My son created a word for never giving up in life. He calls it *pusheverence*—a quality that just won't let you give up! My son has it. I guess he got it from me, and it has been the key to both of our successes. My daughter's too!

Most people play the game of life not to win, but with caution, because of their fear of losing. Don't let fear govern your choices. Create the life you want from the inside out. Start by letting the real you out. Suppose there was a *you* that never got to see the light of day?

Don't be afraid that your life will end. Be afraid that it will never begin. Isn't that a lot more to be afraid of? We don't get to choose how we die, but we do get to choose how we live. Don't live your life with a fear of death. Don't even contemplate death. When it happens, it happens. Contemplate life and how to live it to the fullest while you still have it. If something unforeseen happens, trust yourself enough to know that you will be able to figure out how to deal with any calamity. For instance, if you should fall overboard, don't just keep treading water until you drown. Lie on your back and float as you look at the heavens trusting the universe to take care of you or start swimming for shore once you can see where *there* is.

Life rewards action, but action can sometimes cause accidents. Don't worry about spilling the sauce. It's really how you clean up the mess that makes the difference. Don't languish in lamentations. Ask yourself, *Am I living to suffer or loving to live?* Create an internal picture of what happiness looks like to you and then live that picture every day.

Just as a plane can't fly with ice on its wings, you must free yourself of negativity (ice on your wings) so you can soar. Replace fear with faith, and you'll fly high! Fear pushes you down, faith picks you up. *Let your beliefs be the wind beneath your wings!*

Design a divine you, not a divided you. Become the director in your own life. Unfortunately, most people don't *direct* their lives, they *accept* their lives. Why let your fears flush your life away? Walk out of your past, and climb out of your box by empowering your desires! Then drive in the direction that those desires want to take you.

Remember your inner radiance and how much you love and are

loved. We all love to *be*. When we are threatened with *not being* (death), we immediately realize how much we value *being*. Bask in the joy of just *being*, but risk being the best *you* that *you* can be!

> **Remember, a diamond is just a piece**
> **of coal that stuck to the job!**

9

Be Willing to Risk

The more risks you take, the more mistakes you will make. However, the rewards make all the difference!

To be completely *courageous,* do something *outrageous!* Try something strange for a change!

What risks have you taken lately? What have you failed at? Did you at least attempt enough to have failed at something? You actually risk more by not risking anything at all. You risk not finding out *what could be.* What would you attempt if you knew you could not fail? Have you recently attempted anything? How you spend your days is how you spend your life. Focus on who or what you want to be before it's too late. Remember, it's better to be a *has been* than a *never was.*

Only with risk come rewards. Why not go out on a limb? Isn't that where the fruit is?

What are you willing to do, give up, or change in your life to make your dreams come true? You see, it's not only what your dreams can do for you that matters, it's what you can do for your dreams. *Dreams cost!* They cost money; but more than that, they cost time, sweat, tears, courage, perseverance, and extraordinary patience!

How many of you think that it shouldn't be that way? How

many people think that if God really wanted us to accomplish our dreams, he'd make it easy and comfortable for us? What kind of crazy thinking is that? God never promised any of us an easy life, or there wouldn't be a *purpose* to life. Life is about learning lessons and overcoming obstacles. Even in the Bible, God's *chosen people* had to risk leaving their homes to wander for forty years in the desert before finding their land of milk and honey. Did God make it easy for any of the people in the Bible, whom he loved, like Abraham, Noah, Peter, Mary, or even his own son? They all had trials and tribulations. It was the challenges that they met that tested their mettle. If these people hadn't been put to a test, there wouldn't be a *testament*. The reason these people became great is that they did great things by sticking to their beliefs and overcoming unbelievable obstacles. Did God make life easy for George Washington, Abraham Lincoln, Martin Luther King, Gandhi, or John F. Kennedy? Yet look at what they accomplished!

According to *God* in *Conversations with God*, "There are no real victims in the universe, only creators. The masters who walked this Earth all knew this. No master ever imagined himself to be victimized, even though many were crucified or assassinated."

Decide what it is that you want out of life. Then decide what you are willing to change or sacrifice to get it? Consider all the possibilities and be willing to take responsibility for the outcome. Take credit where credit is due; but you must also be willing to accept blame, if the outcome is not exactly the way you wanted it to be. Unless you are willing to take responsibility for failure, if it occurs, you cannot change any outcome. Instead of fearing failure, learn from failure. Make failure work for you. It is a great fertilizer for dreams! Ask yourself, *"What did I do that resulted in this failure? What lesson can I apply so that it won't happen again?"* If you keep running into brick walls, begin to realize that those walls may not be there to keep you out. Those walls may be there just to give you a chance to show how badly you want something!

When you want something badly enough that there *ain't no mountain high enough* to keep it away from you, you will succeed in getting what you want. The brick walls will crumble when your beliefs and desires become stronger than those walls. Like the Walls of Jericho, those walls will actually fall before your beliefs, but only when your beliefs become strong enough to *topple towers.*

Refuse to lose! Just stay in it until you win it. The people who consistently win are the ones who are willing to take risks to get what they want. Let your desires determine the deadline for your dreams by their intensity. If you're facing an impossible task, act optimistic, like it's impossible to fail. For instance, if you're going fishing but your dream really is to catch Moby Dick, program a positive outcome by bringing along a ton of tartar sauce!

Actually, life is all about attitude. Your attitude really determines your altitude! How high do you think you can go? When ordinary people do extraordinary things, they become heroes. The difference between a *hero* and a *zero* lies in the risks that a hero is willing to take, while the *zero* keeps going around in circles and never leaves *ground zero.* Be the hero in your own life by doing whatever is necessary to get the job done. When you want something in your life badly enough, ask yourself, *"What am I willing to do or give up to get it?"* Be willing to go after what you want consistently and persistently *until* you get it. Sometimes, that may require bending in some very uncomfortable positions. Bend if you have to, but never break!

Bridge the gap between your *want to's* and your *willing to's.* Just because you *want to* doesn't mean anything will change. Unfortunately, you may have to leave your comfort zone and become *willing to* take action to get what you want. There's a design flaw in the universe that makes massages feel better than exercise and chocolate taste better than broccoli. If you constantly make the *feel good, taste good* choice, then you accomplish nothing. Sometimes, success may involve digging your way out of a burrow in order to discover a whole new world at the top. Sadly, though, many of us are willing to dig and dig until we get to daylight; then suddenly, when we see our own shadows, we get frightened and retreat back into our holes. Unlike groundhogs, we shouldn't let our shadows hinder us. We have to be willing to risk and be willing to leave our hole in order to experience a *whole new life.*

It's never crowded along the extra mile, because most people don't go that extra mile. They stop when they get tired, or they let distractions get in their way. There's a saying, *"Don't go where the path may lead, go where there is no path and leave a trail."* Expand your expectations, stretch as far as you can, and turn your growing pains into power! Take a deep breath and visualize yourself becoming an Incredible Hulk that no one can stop!

Align yourself with the greatest possibility for your life, then stay the course as you do whatever it takes to get you there.

There's a story about a man who is standing on a dock waiting for his ship to come in. When nothing happens for a very long period of time, another man standing on the dock next to him just happens to ask, *"I know you are waiting for your ship to come in, but did you send one out?"* How many of us are waiting for our ships to come in, but have never risked sending one out? If you want your ship to come in, you may actually have to send out many ships. Some ships may get caught in a storm or lost at sea. The only way to insure that your ship will come in is to send out many ships and not to just rely on one.

Take a chance while you have the choice. If a crisis should occur, look for the lesson that crisis has provided. Thank the universe for the lesson and move on. You see, it's called a lesson because you're supposed to learn from it, but not to dwell on it. In other words, *if you're going through Hell, don't stop to enjoy the scenery!* Get the hell out of there and go where there is greenery!

If at first you do not succeed, erase all evidence, but keep making the effort. People who consistently win constantly take risks until they do win. Remember, God never promised you a rose garden, and even rose gardens have thorns. What are you willing to do, give up, or be so that the rest of your life can be heavenly?

Decide what you want out of life and go after it. It's not really who you *were* that matters, but who you *become.* You have to be willing to *risk it,* in order to get the *biscuit!*

Rewards are commensurate with the risk you're willing to take.

I remember going to a casino with a friend of mine, who constantly played craps and always won. Since I wanted to be a winner too, I tried doing everything that he did, betting every number he bet. However, my bets were much smaller because I wasn't willing to risk as much. At the end of the evening, my friend came away a large winner (as always), and I came away a loser. How could that have happened when we were betting the same numbers? The difference was that when my friend won, he won big. When I won, I won small because I bet small. My winnings didn't even cover my losses.

Great casinos have been built and fortunes amassed because people seldom walk away winners, but they will walk away when their losses become too great. It is the same with failure. Never walk away as a failure. *Stay in it until you win it.* Your persistence will pay off. Although I am not an advocate of gambling, the same lesson applies to life. How much are you willing to risk to win big? Sometimes, in order to enjoy a great view, you have to be willing to climb higher, even though some of the steps may be shaky.

There's a song by Diana Ross that asks, *"Do you know where you're going to? Do you like what life is showing you?"* If not, it's never too late to start your life over and design the one that you really want. When you live your life *by design,* even *retirement* can be a *refirement* and a take-off instead of a landing.

Procrastination is the thief of time, (our most priceless possession). Don't just let that thief steal your time. Start living your life with intention! As Mattie said, *"Don't die with your music still in you!"* Everyone is meant for some magnificent mission, but each person needs to have a mental map to start their journey. Get juiced! Get going! Since God didn't put an expiration date on any of us, we need to make the best use of every day especially since we don't know which one will be our last. None of us will get out of here alive. Just don't die wondering....

On your deathbed, you will never regret not having spent more time at the office, cleaning your house, or mowing your lawn; but you will regret not having spent more time pursuing your dreams or having fun with your family.

Give up the fear of the unknown and climb out of your comfort zone before it suffocates you. Actually, you must risk going too far to discover how far you can go!

Take the story of two seeds:

Two Seeds (author unknown)

Two seeds lay side by side in the fertile spring soil.

The first seed said, "I want to grow! I want to send my roots deep into the soil beneath me. I want to unfurl my tender buds like banners to announce the arrival of spring. I want to feel the warmth of the sun on my face and the blessing of the morning dew on my petals!" And so she grew!

The second seed said, "I am afraid, I am afraid! If I send my roots into the ground below, I don't know what I will encounter in the dirt. If I push my way through the hard soil above me, I may damage my delicate sprouts. What if I let my buds open and a snail tries to eat them? And if I were to open my blossoms, a small child may pull me from the ground. No, it is much better for me to wait *until it is safe*."

In early spring, a yard hen scratching around in the ground for food found the waiting seed and promptly ate it.

Moral of the story: Those of us who refuse to risk or grow get swallowed up by life!

Don't let this happen to you. Take the wheel! Learn to be the driver in your own life, not just a passenger. Why is it, though, that so many people try to drive forward in life while looking in the rearview mirror? It's okay to check the rearview mirror before you start your drive as a way of looking back and adjusting, but don't use it to drive forward. Don't make your past your future! You might also need to get rid of some of the *junk in your trunk* before moving forward.

If you let it, your past will actually reach into your present and program your future. Since you can't live in two places at one time, why would you choose to live in the past? Only hindsight has 20/20 vision, but don't let your visions of the future be tempered by your past. Instead, live in *the present* and accept the gift that it is. Listen to your own dreams as you step out of the prison of your past into the light of the life you created by design. Actually, it's never too late to even have a happy childhood! Set yourself free to pursue your own passion with vision and power. Become the star in your own life. Maximum results demand maximum you!

A person doesn't always choose the moment that they decide to do something great. Sometimes, the moment chooses the person. Take action when it is called for, but even when it's not. People who refuse to get out of their comfort zones are usually suffocated by them as the sofa sucks them in.

Don't just do things differently, do different things. Get moving! Set sail today. Even if you're heading in the wrong direction, it's easier to get a ship that's already moving to turn around.

Every day, ask yourself what you can do to bring new life to your life—or would you rather just be stuck in your comfort zone?

The Comfort Zone (author unknown)

"I used to have a comfort zone where I knew I could not fail ...
The same four walls and busy work were *really* more like jail ...
I longed so *much* to do the things ... I'd *never* done before ...
But I stayed inside my comfort zone ... and paced the same old floor.
   I *said* it didn't matter ... that I wasn't doing much.
I said I didn't care for things ... like diamonds ... cars ... and such.
I claimed to be so busy ... with the things inside my zone ...
But deep inside ... I longed for ... some *victory* of my own.
   I *couldn't* let my life go by ... just watching *others* win!
I held my breath ... and stepped outside ... to let the change begin ...
I took a step ... and with a strength I'd *never* felt before ...
I kissed my comfort zone good-bye ... and closed and locked ... the door.
   If *you* are in a comfort zone ... afraid to venture out ...
Remember that *all* winners ... at one time ... were filled with doubt ...
A step or two ... and words of praise ... can make *your* dreams come true ...
So greet your future with a smile ... *Success* is there for you!"

Life begins at the end of your comfort zone! Sometimes the best things in life happen after you've done what you're supposed to do. At that point, you're finally free to follow your dreams!

May the most that you wish for be the least that you get.
—Irish proverb

10

Seeking Abundance

Abundance does not refer only to wealth. Abundance can refer to anything you would like to create more of in your life. You might want to create an abundance of love, time, money, energy, joy, or passion. Abundance is really just a state of mind that results in peace of mind. It brings fulfillment. Financial abundance will flow when you can trust yourself enough to create it.

Money is not evil! A lack of money certainly doesn't enrich anyone and can make life pretty miserable. Money, on the other hand, can be used to create the freedom to seek whatever else you would like to have in your life. I always visualize myself as living in *splendid abundance*, and somehow it just flows. Abundance means having more than enough. My attitude has always been that the more I prosper, the more I have to share with everyone else. The more I receive, the more I have to give. It was this belief in splendid abundance and *more* that I used to create *fiscal fitness* in my life. Learning to believe in and create splendid abundance can propel you from poverty into prosperity.

Prosperity is unlimited and is open to all. It has no boundaries! It is okay to be rich, if that is what you choose to be. The universe provides splendid abundance for all those who desire it. Don't consider money as the root of all evil. There are many good things about money and good ways to use your money. Just because you become prosperous doesn't mean someone else has to be poor. That would be true only if there were limited abundance in the universe. Based on a premise of *limited abundance*, if you wanted to add more to your side of the scale, you would have to take from someone else's side of the scale. Abundance doesn't work that way. There is unlimited abundance in the universe, and you can take out as much as you want. Abundance and scarcity are opposites. You can have whichever one you choose, but you can't have both. Everyone doesn't choose the same thing. Some people think that choosing scarcity is a more noble approach, but your choosing to be poor will not make anyone else rich. Choosing unlimited abundance will create enough in your life so that you can give away as much as you want and still have enough left. When you learn how to create unlimited abundance, you will accept only the best that life has to offer. Don't feel unworthy. Just imagine yourself as a satisfied, fulfilled, prosperous person.

After your financial needs are met, true abundance becomes about being able to express your creativity. Don't confuse wealth with freedom. A person doesn't need to be independently wealthy in order to have enough wealth to be independent. Financial abundance will create fiscal fitness, but there are many other kinds of abundance that are more fulfilling. Once your financial needs are satisfied, you can concentrate on those. Abundance is just about having the freedom to pursue the things you love. If you want to be a truly *rich* person, do not wish for just wealth by itself. Wish for a wealth of joy, love, and health.

Having it all together means that your body, mind, and spirit are all aligned. When you want to create *splendid abundance* in your life, imagine the specific details of whatever you want to create. Think in pictures of what an abundant life would look like to you by using an abundance of resourcefulness. Be creative about the details, because the design is in the details.

Seek abundance in everything—love, health, happiness, wealth— everything you want to have in your life. I visualize that I live in splendid abundance and see a horn of plenty constantly spilling out everything I desire in life. The more I take, the more the horn keeps filling itself to overflowing. Focus on what you love and want in your life, then draw that to you. The stronger your emotions are about what you desire, the quicker you will create what you are thinking about.

When you visualize something, you are actually creating it in your imagination. When you believe strongly enough that the image you have created in your mind is real, it will become real—but first only in your imagination. It may take a little more time and effort for that image to manifest into reality for the world to see. Expecting *instant manifestation* is like expecting *instant gratification*. Children expect the latter. Adults realize that something that they really want may take a little longer to create. The important thing is that manifestation does occur. Imagining something repeatedly in your mind actually creates it. A thought begins to take physical form when you imagine it over and over again. By focusing your energy on any one thing, you are literally bringing that thought to life just as Giuseppe did with Pinocchio. Energy creates matter, making whatever energy you put into something not only the cause of your creations, but a catalyst to speed up how quickly they materialize. The more ardently you focus your energy on what you want, the quicker you are actually creating it into reality.

Believing in splendid abundance is like creating an ocean of wealth that you can tap into whenever you want. You can take out a cup full, a bucket full, or a tank full of water from that ocean. Whatever you take out doesn't affect the ocean one bit since the ocean is unlimited. The ocean in no way becomes depleted, no matter how much you take out, because it is always replenishing itself everytime it rains. The ocean doesn't feel the impact of anything that you take out nor does it care. The amount you take out actually is determined not only by what you want but also by what you think you are entitled to. Ironically, you will only take out what you think you deserve. You can take out a whole lot or a whole little. It is entirely up to you, and doesn't actually affect the ocean, which is always full. The universe is always full too. Therefore you can materialize anything you want in your life from the abundance in the universe, and it doesn't deplete the universe.

Wealth is attracted to the person you are in your thoughts! Like attracts like. However, the richest people I know are not the ones with the most money. They are the ones who are rich in love and happiness, which has nothing to do with how much money they have. These people are more interested in fulfillment than in finances and they are constantly attracting love and happiness. The real secret in life is to be able to create enough money to be secure and independent but not so much that all you are living for is the money. Don't confuse money with success. When money becomes your sole focus, you are constantly thinking of how to make more of it, and how to protect it from others. People who focus just on money have to worry about what to do with it, how to hold on to it, and how to keep it safe. Money then becomes a monster which takes over, and, like the plant in *The Little Shop of Horrors*, says *"Feed me, feed me!"*, until it controls your life.

To be in control of your own life, seek happiness, not money, knowing that enough money will always be there to support your happiness if happiness is what you're focusing on. Most people say, *"When I get enough money, I will be happy."* It doesn't work that way. When you focus on happiness instead of money, enough money will materialize to support the happiness which you are creating. When you focus just on money, you will never have enough; and happiness will allude you.

Capitalize on the *wealth within*. That is where your treasure is really stored! As an illustration, consider the following story:

A wise woman, who was traveling in the mountains, found a precious stone sparkling in a stream. Mesmerized by the stone, she picked it up and put in her bag. The next day the woman met another traveler who was hungry; and she opened her bag to share her food. The hungry traveler saw the precious stone and asked the woman to give it to him. She did so without hesitation. The traveler left, rejoicing in his good fortune. He knew the stone was worth a fortune—enough to give him security for a lifetime. However, the next day the man came back to return the stone to the wise woman. The man said to her *"I've been thinking. I know how valuable this stone is, but I give it back to you with the hope that you can give me something even more precious.*

Give me that which is within you that enabled you to give me the stone in the first place!"

When you are visualizing abundance, visualize in feelings and emotions. If you want to be wealthy, focus on what *feeling* you would like to have as a result of that wealth and not just on the money. Money itself is worthless—just pieces of paper that have no intrinsic value. What you want are the feelings that come from what money can buy. You want the feelings of security and peace, the satisfaction of being able to afford to eat a good meal, to live in a great home, the ability to create a comfortable lifestyle, and the freedom to be able to do whatever you want whenever you want to do it. Focus on how you would *feel* if you had an unlimited supply of money. Then create those feelings as if you already had all the wealth you needed. Focus on only positive feelings. You can't get rich by hating poverty! Focus on what you love and want in your life, and then on the feelings that you will have when those things do appear in your life. Don't wish for money, wish for the feelings that are often associated with it. Wish for contentment, independence, security, and joy. Ask yourself, what would those things feel like? Then create those feelings in you own mind. Since they are feelings, you can create them any time you want. Picture how you would feel if you had everything you wanted, and let the universe take care of the details. Act as if those things were *now-here*. Create a picture in your mind. Then put yourself in that picture with all your feelings. Bring in any emotion that that picture would elicit, and turn it up as you would the volume on a TV. Emotion is the power that attracts something to you. It acts like a magnet. Emotion is <u>E</u>nergy in <u>**motion**</u>. A thought is pure energy, but thoughts become creative when you empower them with emotion.

Be the source of your own abundance. Say, *"I am a magnet for splendid abundance. I now attract all that I need and want in my life."* Magnets can only attract like kinds. Did you ever try to attract wood with a magnet? You draw to you whatever you are thinking about. Decide what makes you happy and put more of that in your thoughts and in your life. When you start with a grateful heart, it becomes a magnet that will attract more blessings to you.

Notice a pattern to your pleasures. Don't just stuff more stuff into your life. It should be the feelings and not things that you are after.

Ask yourself, *"Am I really happy?"*

Then picture your life as if it were *bathed in bliss.* Bliss actually comes from your feelings and not your belongings. The things that can make you happy are really *not things,* because *things* can't give you anything back. Yet how many people are controlled by their *belongings?* Belongings are not as important as a *sense of belonging* that occurs when you are surrounded by those you love. It is much more important to put your efforts into instilling love and belonging in the universe than to own any belongings, which are inanimate objects and will not make you happy for very long.

People *stuff* their life with *stuff* and wonder why they still feel empty inside. You can't get long term satisfaction from stuff because stuff can't give back or love back. You can't buy one more outfit, one more pair of shoes, a car, or a house that will make that feeling of emptiness inside of you go away. Give up your need to just have more stuff. After all, if you had *everything,* where would you put it?

Ask yourself, *"What is it that I really want?"* If you're feeling a lack, maybe what's missing in your life is *you!* Happiness is a feeling; and because it is a feeling, it can only come from inside of you. True fulfillment can only be found when you stuff your life with love, serenity, and joy from within knowing that you are connected to a higher source that will create whatever you need in your life whenever you need it.

As you see yourself bathed in bliss, also visualize a silver chalice with a limitless amount of love flowing over the rim. The more you drink from that chalice, the fuller it gets until it just keeps brimming over with love and happiness. Visualize splendid abundance in your life spilling out of a cornucopia that is constantly refilling itself so it cannot be used up. Concentrate on what it would feel like to have a life full of whatever you want. But remember, some of the best things in life cannot be seen or touched. They can only be felt by the heart.

When you start with a grateful heart, it acts as a powerful magnet to attract to you more of that for which you are grateful. Open your heart—let your blessings in and be grateful for what you do have in life. Welcome your blessings and make room for more of them in your life by having an *attitude of gratitude*. Blessings come to where they are appreciated and welcomed and will bring their friends with them. When you look at life through rose-colored glasses, the world changes; and blessings will abound. Don't think of this universe as one of scarcity. Instead, create a strong belief in a universal power that will bring splendid abundance into your life whenever you are ready for it. Then learn how to tap into that fabulous fortune, which is just waiting for you in escrow!

Abundance is limitless, and is actually your birthright. You just need to know how to claim your birthright, which may be hidden from view.

Make a map of just how far and where you are willing to go to find the treasure that is your birthright. Blast through the glass ceiling of your fears into the aliveness and challenge on the other side. Then expand your beliefs to eradicate that ceiling so that you're living a life without limits.

Your beliefs are the key—-the magical combination that will allow you to access the wealth of opportunity that exists all around you. If you don't believe, then the opportunities don't exist. It is your belief that makes them real. Create your beliefs into reality by marrying belief with action. When you believe hard enough, the universe doesn't change; but you change because you have opened yourself up to the possibility of creating whatever you want. Once you have pondered the possibility, prepare for the probability by visualizing whatever you want until it materializes.

Remember, the universe is a source of wealth. All you have to do is tap into it and take out whatever you decide you want —whether it be a spoonful, a cup full, a bucket full, or even an ocean full! The amount you take out is up to you and is determined by what you think you are worthy of. Your beliefs will only let you take out what you think you should have. If what you have now is not enough for you, you must expand your beliefs until what you have is enough.

Your self-worth is actually a by-product of your self-concept. Change your self-concept, and your net worth will soon match your new self-worth. Work on yourself first—your belief in who you are.

Then, like in *The Field of Dreams*, if you build the field, *they will come.* Just build the field. Whatever you want will *automagically* appear when *your belief becomes stronger than your fear.* Your mind is such fertile soil. Plant the seeds of belief that will grow and materialize. Everything sprouts from your visions and beliefs! You cannot create outside of you what you cannot visualize inside of you.

You are not what you *acquire;* but you are what you *achieve.* Your ability to be resourceful at just receiving abundance (as in inheriting), rather than achieving abundance, diminishes that abundance because it is not accompanied by a sense of accomplishment and pride. *Achieving abundance,* which you derive from your own efforts, is much more rewarding. When you start with a strong belief in yourself and a strong belief in an abundant universe, miracles will occur, especially when you marry your beliefs with action!

When I was young, I grew up poor in materialistic things; but I never felt deprived. Somehow, whatever I needed was always there for me whenever I needed it. However, I didn't like the concept of being *poor* because I felt I was worth more. *Poor* is who I was, not who I am. When I discovered the magic in my beliefs, my reality began to conform with the vision I had of how I wanted my life to be. I also had the added satisfaction of having achieved success on my own.

Life is a learning process. As you learn *more,* you can conceive of *more.* As you conceive of *more* and believe in *more,* you can create *more.* *More* is good. *More* means different things to different people. *More* can refer to *more* love, *more* happiness, or *more* wealth. *More* can be whatever you want it to be. Invite *more* into your life by envisioning what you would like to have *more* of, and then start believing that *more* is already here. "*Gimme more, gimme more, gimme more!*" Be grateful when *more* shows up in your life. Keep creating *more* until you are totally filled, and then give the surplus away so that even *more* can come into your life.

Celebrate other people's good fortune also by believing that you have an invisible connection to everything in the universe. After all, we are all connected to source energy, which creates everything in the universe. Don't make calling your source a long distance call because you have moved away from it. Constantly reconnect yourself with source energy so it is where you are. A great force comes from your connection to your source. When you connect with your source, you actually become a *sorcerer* and, as such, can benefit from the *magical* power to create. Use that power to benefit yourself and others. We are all part of that same tree (source energy) and have common roots, although we may branch out in different directions. Always stay connected to your source, no matter how high your branches may grow. Don't let your branches snap off and become disconnected from their source, or they will die.

People think in pictures, then act out the pictures that they have created in their minds. Everybody has a different picture of what they desire. For instance, some people might picture a *porch* and some a *Porsche*. We all tend to choose pictures that make us feel good and to move away from the pictures that make us feel bad because, basically, we all want to feel good. Once we believe that we are worthy of happiness, we can create what that happiness looks like in our life. Just as when you look at a doughnut, you should focus on the dough and not on the hole; you should focus on what you have in your life right now that makes you happy, not on what you don't have. When you are satisfied with what you have, you become rich. When you think about what you don't have, you will think of yourself as poor. It's actually all in your mind. Dwell on the things that you are happy about in your life. Then visualize the things you still want but do not have currently. See them coming into your life. A positive thought has to occur first before something can materialize, so only think about what you want.

Once you have formulated your desires and tapped into the infinite source, you need to *believe* that everything you have ever needed or wanted is already here for you. Actually, you can believe any desire into being. It's all about the *belief!*

There are two words that are not in my vocabulary—lack and scarcity. Since the universe provides everything I need, there is no reason to use either of these words. There is no lack of anything in my life. Everything that I want, such as love, family, friends, success, food, clothes, shoes, are all ample and abundant in my life. (I am not bragging—I am creating!) My pantry and freezer are always full, and I lack for nothing—not even time. As one of my friends once said to me, *"How come you have thirty hours in your day?"* It's because I created my life that way!

Time is the most valuable thing I have in my life, and how I choose to spend my time is up to me. I want to spend as many minutes in joy and happiness as I can. You can always create more money, but you can't create more time. That is why time is even more valuable than money. Spend each hour of each day as wisely as if each hour was a thousand dollar bill. After all, what is worth more than this moment? Live in the moment. Enjoy each moment, and moment by moment, you will create a happy life for yourself!

Don't let situations steal your joy. Our happiness really depends not on our circumstances, but on our disposition at the moment. Instead of being upset about someone or something and living your life with anxiety and anger, let positive thoughts transport you to a different space and a different place where you can find peace and happiness.

Go *within*, and you will never do *without*. Meditate each day and order your soul's desire. Actually, it is today's special on the menu! Use your desires not only to enrich your life, but to enrich the lives of others. It is very hard to get rich yourself without enriching others.

You can either wish big and have it all, or you can wish small. You can even not wish at all! Either way, the universe gives you what it thinks you want. The wish is up to you! If you think small, and therefore wish small, you will stay small. If you think and wish *big or tall*, you can have it all! The results you generate are what you think you deserve.

This is a universe of energy and attraction. Keep your thoughts focused on what you intend to create and make yourself available for success. Don't relate to scarcity in anything. Believe that everything you need will be available to you when you need it because you now know how to create it. Experience what you want in your mind first before it shows up, and then act as if everything you desire were already here. Since you cannot create outside of you what you cannot visualize inside of you, the things that you want have to start in your head first as visualizations. Also know that you can't create something unless you really believe that it will happen. Your belief is the key! Expand your expectations and your beliefs. Since the power is within you to be anything you want to be and to have anything you want to have in you life, all you have to do is harness that power to grow into greatness!

Yearn, baby, Yearn!

11

Color Outside the Lines!

How many people think it is important to color within the lines?

As a child, most of us are taught to color within the lines and are proud of ourselves when we can do so. However, when a person colors within the lines, that person is actually filling in on someone else's picture. Why not dare to go outside the lines? Better yet, why not draw your own lines and fill them in with pretty pastels, instead of dark dismal colors?

Each day, the universe provides an empty easel with a blank sheet of paper on it. You are the artist. What are you going to draw today? Will it be a happy day filled with joy and love, or a dreary day filled with disappointment and dismay? Worst yet, if you decide to draw an unhappy picture today, will it be the same picture that you painted yesterday? How many people are in the habit of only displaying disasters because that's what they are thinking about? Instead, learn to be a *master of the mirage!* See only what you want to see happen. If you want to change your life, start by changing your mental pictures.

Every day, draw on the *canvas of could be* what you would want your day to look like. Fill in the picture with lots of details and bright colors. Fixate on that picture in your mind, and then maintain that picture mentally throughout the day. Create your day so that real life mimics your art. Remember, though, that you can never create your own individual masterpiece if you are using a *paint by numbers* kit. Be *U-nique!*

Don't paint the same picture every day 365 days a year, because then you're living the same day over and over. If your picture is not happy, get a new canvas, and create a memorable masterpiece. Be your own Michelangelo, with a little inspiration from above. Paint what you might see when your inner child comes out to play and create a magical kind of day!

Don't get caught up with the external framework of the picture. When you're dusting the picture or focusing on the frame, you don't really see the picture. Visualize the entire picture in your mind before you create it on canvas. Then put yourself inside the canvas and live that picture.

Each day, there is not only a brand new canvas in your life but an endless supply of multicolored paint. Paint anything you want, but make it colorful, fun, and memorable. If you don't know what to paint, try experimenting with finger painting and a picture will emerge. The picture is really inside of you. What will today look like? That's up to you. I create what I call *delicious days*, at least once a week, when I can do whatever I want to do that day and not what I have to do.

Paint the picture of your life as if you had control over your life. What would your life look like if you had complete control over it? Each day, events do occur that we have no control over, but what we do have control over is our *reaction* to those events.

Since there are no accidents in the universe, everything that happens in life is either a *lesson* or a *blesson*. The only difference between those two words is a "b," and the "b" stands for <u>b</u>elief. Your beliefs can turn even the hardest *lessons* into *blessons*, depending upon your interpretation. Sometimes a *lesson* is really a *blesson* in disguise. When you realize that you can control your interpretation of any situation, you can actually take control of that situation. It should not be the other way around where that situation takes control of you and elicits anger or bad feelings within you.

Sometimes bad things do happen to good people, although it is really a person's interpretation of an event that makes it permanently good or bad in their life. An event is just an event and is emotionally neutral; but sometimes when an event has to do with our homes, our health or our family, our emotions create the consequences. Just know that everything happens for a reason, and that you are strong enough to handle whatever may come along. When a storm does occur in your life, you can curse the storm and wait impatiently for it to pass; or you can learn to dance in the rain. The choice is up to you. No matter what is happening outside, you can always choose to be in touch with your own inner source of happiness and project that happiness on to others. Once you fall into the flow of inner felicity, you will become absorbed in what you're doing; and outside influences will have little if any effect on you.

Since happiness is a choice, why not choose happiness? Wrap yourself in a blanket of inner happiness, and let it give you emotional insulation from the rest of the world.

Happiness is unique to each individual since it has a different definition for everyone. What makes one person happy might be barely tolerable for another. My dog's definition of happiness, which is a pat on the head and a good bone, would certainly not make me very happy.

Sometimes happiness has to do with how we look at things. Things are what they are, but they become what we make them. By focusing on the wrong things, we can actually block our own happiness. This point was brought home to me recently. It was a lesson from the universe, for which I was grateful.

My husband and I were spending the weekend at our Ocean City condo, after our condo association had made it mandatory for all unit owners to replace all the sliding glass doors in each unit. Since we have seven pairs of sliding glass doors in our unit, this was quite expensive. Also, I did not like the new doors that were selected to withstand hurricanes because the frames were much thicker, bulkier, and darker than the old ones. One of the many joys I have always experienced at our condo is when the universe mysteriously wakes me up at the crack of dawn each morning so that I can witness a sensational sunrise— from my bed! I am not a morning person and never wake up to see a sunrise other than down the ocean.

On the first morning after the new doors were installed, sure enough the universe woke me up on time; but I could not see the sunrise because the thicker frames of the new doors were in the way, blocking my view. Because I was focusing my attention on the frames, I became angry and upset, blaming the frames for stealing my sunshine. Then suddenly, I realized that if I just changed my position, while still in bed, I could see the sunrise. You see, the sun was still there, where it had always been; but I was focusing so hard on the frames that I almost missed it. A simple *shift in position* brought my sunshine back and allowed me to forget the frames. What I learned from this experience was that something external can't block your happiness, *unless you let it!*

Happiness has to start from within an individual and then flow outward. It comes from the way we look at life by dwelling on our benefits and blessings and not on our misfortunes. To illustrate this point, I'd like to relate two stories about actual customers of mine, which I think will demonstrate what I am talking about. I happened to have two different listing appointments with previous clients on the same day. Their lives had dramatically changed over the years, although I didn't know it until I showed up for the appointments.

My first client was a lawyer, who, several years earlier, was at the peak of his career—very successful and happily married with two daughters. He owned a lovely home in my area, plus one in Ocean City, and was also building a retirement home in Florida, when he started experiencing health problems. Diagnosed with neuropathy, which gradually progressed into an immune deficiency, his health went progressively downhill to the point where he had a myriad of things wrong with him—bad knees, high blood pressure, hardening of the arteries, and so on. From the moment I entered this man's front door, I was presented with a barrage of negativity, which started with his sharing all his health problems with me and progressed into how all builders in Florida were crooks, how he hated his mother because she never wanted him (she wanted a girl!), and finally into how his marriage was dissolving.

This client and I had already spent the first fifteen minutes of my appointment looking for his cell phone. He actually thought that a magazine sales lady, whom he had invited into his home before me, had stolen it. Obviously, he was quite upset, until he found the phone right where he had lost it—in his front bushes. That day also happened to be this client's thirteenth wedding anniversary; but sadly, he and his wife had just separated. The wife remained in Florida by herself although they had sent each other flowers that day. I spent about ten minutes talking about the sale of this man's house (which unfortunately had gone down in value from the height of the market two years earlier), and two hours listening to him complain about everything that was wrong in his life. I have never been surrounded by so much negativity. Absolutely drained by the experience, I couldn't wait to get out of the door. No wonder this man's body was falling apart! He had internalized everything that was wrong in his life and fed his body nothing but negativity—a potential poison!

According to this man, everyone in his life was trying to take advantage of him—doctors, salesmen, builders, and even buyers! His beliefs were poisoning him, but he chose to take another dose of destruction each day. It was like this man had a cloud of negativity hanging over his head wherever he went. This poor man could not see the sunshine, but heard only the thunder and storms. There was, indeed, a cloud with a string on it following this man, but make no mistake about who was pulling the string to make that cloud follow him everywhere. Unfortunately, this client took no responsibility whatsoever for the storms in his life. Blaming everyone else, including his mother and God, for his lack of sunshine, this man could not see that he was creating clouds every day by always dwelling on the negative. What was wrong with his life? Everything!

Since negative things were all he could talk about, the universe must have thought that was what he wanted to create. Mishandled misfortune manufactures more misfortune, and that was what he got. Unfortunately, this client could not see what a negative spiral he was on or what he was creating in his life. Instead, he chose to wallow in despair, never smiling, just walking around with permanent PMS (Poor Me Syndrome)! The universe just kept pouring even more troubles on this drowning man. I guess that the universe actually thought he wanted to drown based on his thoughts!

Once I realized I couldn't get through to this man enough to help him (his clouds were too thick), I couldn't wait to get out of there, go home, and wash my own mind. I did not want to catch his contagious condition!

My next listing appointment that day was with other another previous client, whom I had not seen in many years—a very nice-looking young couple with two teenage children. The man had not told me, prior to our meeting, that he too had suffered a real tragedy. He had had his leg amputated as a result of a car accident, that was not his fault. When I saw this client with a prosthetic leg, I was shocked. Then this client told me (only casually) that he had also lost his ambulance business as a result of the accident and wanted to sell the home that housed it. My heart went out to him! The whole time he was telling me this, however, he had a big smile on his face and a loving wife by his side. His life had also tragically changed because of circumstances beyond his control, but he had accepted his fate, maintained that life was good, kept a big smile on his face, and was actually learning to drive with one leg. This man had a very positive attitude about life, never once wallowing in self-pity. At the end of the interview, I hugged this client. I came home feeling inspired by this man's spirit and really wanting to help him. I will never forget the smile on his face, and I worked hard to keep it there.

I did sell his property, but not without problems. A home inspection created a need for a new furnace and many other costly repairs. A week before settlement, his property was also seriously damaged by a hit-and-run driver, causing even more problems. Undaunted, this client got through each hurdle and acted as if it was nothing. He was always upbeat and positive. No one was going to steal this man's sunshine because it was in his heart. What a contrast these two clients were! After settlement, the second client wrote a glowing report about the service I had rendered, but I really wanted to thank him for his inspiration, which was so uplifting in my life. (Thank you, Tony! You have inspired me!)

Which of these two people do you think the world would rather be around? Who is creating the best future for himself, despite adversities?

Rain falls on all of us periodically. No one is immune. All we can do is learn how to benefit from the rain as well as how to create sunshine in our lives.

Adversity does occur, but it is actually our *attitude about adversity* that determines how long the storm will last. A bad attitude can cripple us more than any handicap or physical defect. When we hit troubled waters, we can just let the storm sink our boats; or we can change course and sail on to safer waters.

Remember, your future can be determined by *choice or chance*. The choice is up to you. You can choose to be the person who changed because of what happened to you (by becoming bitter) or the person who changed because of what you chose to do about what happened to you (by becoming stronger and more accepting). Choose to get better and not to be bitter. Turn your pain into power! Become a *hippo of happiness* rather than a *porcupine of pain*! Since happiness is a feeling, pretend that you are happy; and you will be. Pretend you are well, and you will be. Since thoughts transform into things, we become what we think about the most. Make your life a *pursuit of happiness*.

The people in life who are the happiest don't always have the best of everything, but rather they make the best of everything they have. It's really quite simple. When you don't have what you want—just resolve to want what you have! Opening your heart with an attitude of gratitude will cause you to attract more blessings and good things in your life. You will be amazed at what will come in if you are just open to the possibility.

How have you moved in the direction of your dreams since last year? What would have to happen in the next three years for your life to be totally fulfilled and happy? Are you working on that? Paint that picture. Make it a *work of heart*! Capture your picture on canvas? Then go out and make your real life mirror your art!

Positive pictures are priceless, because they don't get lost like tears in the rain!

12

J. O. Y.

The best way to find joy is to *Just Open Yourself!*

Joy is all around you if you're open enough to let it in. Joy does not come and go, it is always there; but the awareness of it comes and goes. Joy needs no reason, it is just simply there. Find that place deep inside of you where joy and happiness reside. Then let that joy permeate your life. To create joy, all you have to do is switch to the J.O.Y. channel, blocking out all the others. Sign up for serendipity. It's cheaper than FIOS!

The opposite of joy is misery. Misery is the feeling of being unfulfilled, which comes from failing to experience who and what you are. Why do so many people choose to create misery when what they really want to create is joy?

How do you create joy? Go back to the core of happiness and peace inside of you that we were all born with. Take time to play and discover like a child. What did you enjoy doing as a child? Put the fun back into your life. Decide what it is that makes you happy and put more of that into your life. Notice when you are the happiest. What are you doing? Who are you with? What are you doing when time just flies? What are you experiencing that makes you feel the happiest inside? Notice where your joy is and put more of <u>you</u> there.

Sometimes, happiness can be found not by changing your address, but just by changing your mind. When you change your mind, you change your future. After all, how could things get better if nothing ever changed?

Life is out there and is ready whenever you are. Your purpose in life is whatever you say it is. It is up to you to create excitement and passion for your purpose, so that it will become contagious. Only one person can be in charge of your bliss. That person is *you*. Happiness isn't about how much money you have to spend, but rather about how you spend your time. Ask yourself, *"How can I make a career out of doing what I love?"* Joy comes from within, not from without. When we search for joy in external things like a new car, one more pair of shoes, a new house, or the right partner, we will never find it. When we discover joy from within, all of these things can flow into our lives and enhance our joy; but they cannot create the joy that is inherent in all of us.

If you think that it is impossible to find joy within yourself, then you will not find it elsewhere. Why search for something outside of you that is already within you? That is simply self-neglect. Instead, recognize the joy that is already inside of you. Discover it, talk about it, dwell on it. What you perceive, you project. For instance, when someone asks you, *"How are you?"* do you mindlessly just say, *"Fine"*, or do you say, *"Super, great, joyful, exhilarated, ecstatic!?"* (An agent on The Northrop Team actually answered that question by saying, *"If I were a dog, my tail would be wagging!"*) You feel what you say you're feeling, and you are how you say you are. Some people would answer that same question with, *"Terrible, awful, humdrum, or just okay."* If your answer is, *"I am the same as yesterday, no better, no worse,"* you are telling your body it's okay to feel the same as yesterday, no better, no worse. Don't you want to feel better than yesterday? Why not try? Even just a smile has been known to produce endorphins which will make you feel better. You are constantly creating your physical condition by conditioning your thought process. What you say is what you create. *Speak up for serendipity!* Words have power—even unspoken words, that only your mind hears! From our conversations (even with ourselves) come affirmations.

Our thoughts are so powerful that even our health can be affected by our thoughts. We have all heard the term *psychosomatic*, which implies that an illness which is not real can be created in someone's mind until the symptoms become real. If we can cause ourselves to become sick by our thoughts, we can also cause ourselves to heal through our thoughts. This was proven very poignantly through a personal experience of mine. Several years ago, my husband was diagnosed with prostate cancer and had to undergo radiation treatment to help cure the illness. The treatment worked, but the effects of the radiation took their toll. My husband was actually reliving this illness over and over every day in his thoughts. Each day was filled with multiple doctor appointments and ramifications from the radiation. By living this illness in his mind and dwelling on it, my husband was actually recreating the illness each day, until his life became about his illness. I finally asked my husband what it would take to get his mind off the illness and for him to get well. Half jokingly, he said, "*Well, if I had a 1959 Cadillac convertible, I could get well*", never dreaming that I would go along with it. To his surprise, I said, "*If you can find a 1959 Cadillac convertible, it's yours, but only if you get well!*"

There was an immediate difference in my husband's expression, his thoughts, and his life! He started to get excited and passionate about the car, spending his days trying to locate a very special Cadillac, to bring it here, to find parts for it, and to restore it once he found it. Since he didn't have time to think about his illness anymore; miraculously, it just went away. Two years later, my husband is completely cancer free! Even the effects of the radiation have disappeared. Furthermore, his 1959 Cadillac convertible, which he rebuilt from the inside out, has won first place in every national automobile show it has been in. That's what positive thoughts can do! How you think and what you hear yourself saying in your mind can make all the difference in how you feel.

So, — *Hears* -to-Your-Health!

Many people want to learn the *how* of happiness. Actually, it's not about the *how* of happiness. It's about the *now* of happiness. Instead of looking to find happiness, like it's somewhere outside of you, just bring it with you. Happiness is a choice. It is how you choose to think. Once you realize that the choice is yours, why not choose happy thoughts rather than letting unhappy thoughts choose you? Who is in control here, anyway?

In order for your life to be wonderful, ask yourself, *"What would an ideal day look like to me? Where would I have to live and with whom?"* Then ask yourself, *"Why aren't I there right now? What's stopping me?"*

Happiness is *not* about the *not now* or *not yet*. It's about the *now*. Choose happiness *now*!

Decide what it is that you're passionate or excited about and put more of that into your life. If you're passionate about nothing, you have no life at all. Passion is the path to self-actualization. Passion makes your dreams possible. Many of your dreams may at first seem impossible, and then they may seem improbable. However, if you believe in those dreams passionately, they will soon become inevitable. Plant your dreams, water and fertilize them, and miracles will grow. You always get what you create, and you are always creating. You don't always get what you want, but you always get what you are picturing in your mind. Imagination is that powerful!

All thought is creative, even a thought that says *I do not want this*. Because the subconscious is pure energy, it can only deal positively with the pictures that you program into it. Since the subconscious doesn't understand the concept of *not*; it can only create what you are picturing, whether that picture is what you want or not. Your subconscious actually does everything it can to manifest your mental pictures since it is the job of the subconscious to transform your thoughts into reality. However, the subconscious is not an author, an editor, or a director. It is a Zerox. It can only *copy* the pictures you give it. The subconscious really cannot understand why you would plant pictures in your mind and thoughts of things that you do not want, but it is not the job of the subconscious to understand or interpret. The subconscious has one job, and that job is to duplicate your thoughts into reality.

Thought is powerful! It excites energy when it is turned on; but like a copier, the subconscious can only copy what it is given. A copier can't criticize, question, or change any text. It is *a copier!* Knowing that you're dealing with such a powerful machine like your mind, which duplicates any copy it is given, why would you put a thought into it that you don't want replicated into reality? You are the creator, author, and editor of your thoughts. If you want better reality, give your subconscious better copy! Are you happy with the results that your current thoughts are producing? If not; then wherever you are, it's the right place and the right time to change them! Changing your thoughts may be the only way you can live *happily even after.*

When you are happy with yourself and your life, you have created a self that needs no improvement. Why then can't you just relax and enjoy life?

Suppose, one morning, you woke up and heard the following:

"Good morning. This is God speaking. Since I will be handling all of your problems today, I do not need your help. Just go out and have a nice day!"

Could you then let yourself be happy, knowing that the universal power was handling all the details?

Accepting that the universe can sometimes trump your desires is hard, but everything happens for a reason. Sometimes the universe gives us more than we could ever dare to hope for. When that happens, just go with the flow! Sometimes, the universe doesn't give us what we ask for, but gives us what is best for us (although we may not know it at the moment). We think our prayers are not being answered when the truth is that sometimes what we are praying for is not in our best interests. Sometimes, God doesn't answer our prayers in just the way we want him to because he has something better in mind. Looking at things as we do from an ant's eye view of the world is not the same as looking at things through a wizard's view of the universe.

It has been said that God is weaving the tapestry of our lives into a beautiful picture; but sometimes, looking at the tapestry from our viewpoint underneath, all we can see are the loose threads and the knots. Trust the all-knowing universe that the picture, when looked at with the right side up, will be perfect. It's important to let the universe know what you desire, but then let the *Master-Craftsman* decide on the details and weave the picture.

Occasionally, when things do go wrong in our lives, we may ask ourselves, *"What did I do to deserve this?"* Sometimes, it is just a lesson that we needed to learn. Lessons at times may taste bitter and be very unpleasant until we discover what purpose they serve.

There is an analogy in a story about a teenager who comes home one day, complaining to her mother about everything that has gone wrong in her life. The daughter is very upset that she failed a test that day, that her boyfriend broke up with her, and that her best friend announced she was moving away. The mother, in sympathy, suggests that she bake her daughter a cake to make her feel better.

"Thanks, Mom. I love your cakes."

"Perhaps then you can help me. I'll need you to sample along the way. Here, have some cooking oil."

"Yuck," says her daughter.

"How about a couple of raw eggs?"

"Gross, Mom!"

"Would you like some flour then, or maybe some baking soda? How about some vanilla?"

"Mom, those are all yucky! What are you trying to do to me?"

The mother replies, "I am just trying to get you to understand. All of those ingredients may taste bad by themselves, but when they are put together in the right way, they make a wonderfully delicious cake!"

God works in much the same way. We may question him and wonder why he would let his children experience bad and difficult times, but God sees the bigger picture. He knows when all these things are put together in the right combination, something good will come out of it. We just have to trust him; and in a little while, something wonderful will show up. I remember when my first marriage was ending, I prayed for it to mend. I did not know that there was something much better around the bend! Later on, I realized how blind I had been, but only when something so much better showed up for me. God was simply clearing the clutter in my life so I could find out what true happiness was all about. Sometimes, we are unwilling to let go of the status quo, which we think is our safety net. However, in order to fly, we have to be willing to leave terra firma and trust the universe.

Just as parents would not let their children play with matches or ride their bikes into a busy street, sometimes God has to say *"no"*. What we want to have happen in our lives may not be what is best for us. There's an old saying that, *"if you want to make God laugh, show her your plans!"* When God says *"no"*, it's not because *she* doesn't love us. It's because she loves us so much that she wants us to be happy and to find the right way. God always gives us what is best for us, but not always what we ask for, especially if what we ask for is not right for us. Sometimes it is just the timing that is wrong. Remember, only God can see the broader picture of what's in store for us in the future. Just as parents would serve a child broccoli for dinner instead of french fries until that child is old enough to make good choices on his own, sometimes divine intervention has to take over. Until we can learn to make proper choices and to choose what is best for us on our own, some *GUIDANCE BY GOD* has to take place. Always remember that God loves us and wants us to be happy. That's why He sends us a beautiful sunrise in the morning and a sunset in the evening. Just think, God can live anywhere in the universe that he chooses to live, but he chooses to live in our hearts! Make sure that yours is a happy place for God to dwell.

If you define happiness as something that you have to *chase* or *catch*, you will search for it outside of you. If happiness were outside of you, then love would be too; and it would not be something that you could feel. Stop chasing happiness as if it is something you can catch. Instead of chasing happiness as if it were *somewhere out there* beyond you, stand still and let happiness catch up with you, realizing that it comes from within. You see, *ever since happiness heard your name, it has been running through the streets trying to find you!* Just open the door and say, *"Here I am!"* Happiness will float in. Make happiness feel at home; and it will stay forever, if you want it to. Can you think of a better roommate? In the meantime, force yourself to smile, if you have to, because a smile is a curve that sets everything straight. Since a smile produces endorphins, which actually make you feel better, it's impossible to think unhappy thoughts with a smile on your face. Smiles are contagious, and lifting another person's spirit is the nicest way to get high that I can think of!

Tell yourself, *"I will employ only happy thoughts in my mind. All others need not apply!"* Every event has a gift, and in each experience is hidden a treasure. Look for that treasure. The key to future happiness is happiness in the present. Why postpone happiness when it is possible to enjoy happiness now and also to take it with you into the future. That way you will never be without happiness.

There was a belief among the ancient Egyptians, who built the pyramids and believed in multiple gods. When a soul passed on to go to its afterlife, the gods would ask two questions to determine the value of the life that that soul had lived while here on Earth. The two questions that the gods would ask were: *"Did you find joy in your life?* and *Did you bring joy to other people's lives?"* What more important reasons are there for living a lifetime than to experience joy and to bring joy to others? The questions that the gods, in their wisdom, asked weren't about how much wealth you had acquired, where you lived, what kind of chariot you drove, or how famous you were. *Joy* was the barometer, the yardstick, the greatest commodity on Earth! How much better off would we be in modern times if we used *joy*—ours and what we can bring to others—as the measure of our lives? Wouldn't we then be living each day in ecstasy, enjoying each sunrise, storm, and sunset instead of uttering shoulda's and coulda's that cloud our thinking?

Since happiness has a different definition for everyone, ask yourself, *"What does happiness look like to me?"* Since your happiness is unique to you, only you can determine what will make you happy. To a dog, happiness is a bone, a pat on the head, or perhaps just your coming home! What is happiness to you? What makes your tail wag? Don't be too general. If you want to recapture what happiness feels like to you, remember that happiness is an emotion. It is what you are feeling. Trust your emotions. They are like envoys relaying a message of what is going on inside of you.

Think in emotions or feelings. Don't just think of things that would make you happy, like a new car or a prestigious job, because cars deteriorate and jobs can end in lay-offs. Think of the feelings that those things would bring if you had whatever you wanted in your life, and don't just limit yourself to a job or a car. If what you really want is to feel proud of yourself, to feel content, important, and secure, those are feelings that you can create even without the job or the car.

Instead of trying to climb the corporate ladder, climb the creative ladder. Once you find your happy place inside of you based on your feelings, no one can take that away from you. When you think abundantly and happily, energy flows into that thought and turns it into an intention. Instead of wishing for money to bring you happiness, just let happiness in, and let it bring you money. Even if it doesn't, you will end up with happiness, which is the result you wanted in the first place!

Be your own happiness boss!

How do you define your joy? Do you have a *joy zone* that you can discover? Let your inner fountain of feelings flow freely as you get enmeshed in your own inner inklings. When you look for happiness outside of you by comparing yourself to or competing with others, you will never be happy. There will always be someone who is smarter, prettier, luckier, or richer by comparison. Don't be envious. What other people have has nothing to do with you. Be happy for them. When you fall into the flow of your own inner happiness, there is no one there to compete with. *Contentment is self-contained.* Mentally, fill your own chalice first and then give away the overflow. If your chalice is empty, you have nothing to give away to others. *Aspire to inspire!*

Look for the best in others, and that will bring out the best in you. Instead of criticizing others, try imagining them being better than they are. Imagine another person having the best attributes they could possibly have, and then encourage that person to exercise those attributes. As those attributes actualize, that other person will attribute them to you. There is no better way to perfect your potential than to help others around you to grow. Other people will be magnetized by you and want to be around you. Your popularity will soar, and everyone will want to be your friend.

At present, do your friends thank you for being in their lives? Actually, people don't choose their friends for what they look like or who they are on the outside; they choose their friends for the way that they feel when they are with them. Think about your friends that you love the most. If your friends are supportive, approving, and inspiring because of their love for you, you will go out of your way to be with them. It's kind of like how we feel about being with our dogs. We don't really choose to be with our dogs for their intelligence or good looks. Instead, we choose to be with our dogs because of the way we feel around them when they lavish all their excitement, attention, and unconditional love on us. Even if we discipline our dogs and scold them, they will still love us unconditionally. Imagine being that kind of friend and wagging your tail in happiness when a friend of yours walks into a room!

A really good friend is one who makes you feel good about yourself! People love to be around other people who make their hearts happy. These people are known as *feel-good buddies* or <u>Heart-Happy Humans</u> (*HHHs*)! Get a good dose of HHHs every day because heart-happy humans are actually heart healthy!

The opposite of this type of person is a hostile human (HH). These humans can be most uncomfortable to be around. No one wants to be around someone who is critical and hostile all the time. Most people will actually go out of their way to avoid hostile humans. When you surround yourself with the 3 Hs and learn to stay away from the 2 Hs, your life will be a lot happier. Identify the heart- happy-humans in your life and make a conscious effort to be around them as often as you can. Also try to be an HHH to as many people as you can.

Hostile humans are not happy humans and cannot stand to be around HHHs. Beware, HHs are actually envious of the happiness that HHHs have and will try to suck happiness from them, much as a vampire would suck their blood. Since HHs cannot find happiness within themselves, they try to steal it from others. When this doesn't work, HHs try to ruin the happiness of others so they can seem happier by comparison. HHs will always do something to try to spoil the fun of others since they cannot stand the fact that everyone else but them is having a good time. Instead of letting happiness flow, especially knowing that it might be contagious, HHs will always find something to criticize and be unhappy about. No one can change HHs, who have actually chosen to be as they are. Joy is alien to them. All HHHs can do is to guard their own happiness and choose not to be around hostile humans, who love to ruin holidays, parties, and family celebrations. Insulate your own heart by wrapping it in a blanket of inner happiness to protect it, and avoid hostile humans whenever you can.

Is there a chance that HHs could change? Yes ... but in order to do that, they would have to add another H to their name. That H stands for happiness, which can only come from inside of them. Unfortunately, that is the last place that HHs would look, preferring instead to try to take happiness from others. Hoard your happiness when dealing with these hostile humans. We may not be here for a long time, but we should certainly be here for a good time. Be a heart-happy human to as many people as you can. Making other people feel good about themselves is the best way to feel good about yourself. Focus outward once you have found your own happiness within.

There are some people who believe that a person can't have happiness without suffering for it. They believe that there is a price to pay for happiness. These people somehow mistakenly believe that getting a *PhD in pain* will make them happier, or at least more worthy of happiness. That is just plain wrong! Happiness doesn't have to be deserved or earned. It is free! There is not even a happiness tax or VAT that you have to pay! — At least, not yet!

Pleasure is different from happiness. Pleasure is a response to a stimulus. There has to be a catalyst that activates pleasure, like a good meal, a good movie, or a good lover. Happiness just is. It is a state of being—not in response to anything—just being.

Make happiness your drug of choice. It doesn't cost anything to snort happiness. It is not against the law to get a *happiness high*, and it is actually good for you. Keep sniffing as you breathe in happiness. Once you have found that state of nirvana inside of you, decide to stay there and share it with others.

Have you had your *happiness fix* for today? Happiness starts from within but actually radiates outward and generates more happiness. Be a *happiness carrier* and be glad that it is contagious. Your friends won't always remember what you had to say, but they will always remember how they feel when they're around you.

When you look for the good in others that is exactly what you will find. Ask yourself, *"Who did I see or talk to today? Did I leave their lives a little happier for my having been in it? Can I manage to do that everyday?"* Wouldn't your life be happier if you concentrated on enhancing the lives of others instead of constantly criticizing others, which only invites their criticism in return?

Some people may think it is more fun to try to improve other people by criticizing them than it is to improve themselves. These foolish people believe they are on a mission to improve others. Here's a newsflash! You can't change other people or improve them by criticizing them. You have to either accept them the way they are or move on. The only thing you can change is your judgment of them.

Remember, that the people who are the happiest in life are not the ones who have the best of everything, but the ones who make the best of everything they have. That doesn't mean that everything is perfect in their lives. It simply means that these people can see beyond the imperfections. These are the people who make up their minds that they are going to like whatever happens to them because they look for the benefits in any situation. When one doesn't dwell on imperfections, even a flawed diamond can still be beautiful and valuable.

Why do *bad* things happen to *good* people? Actually, nothing is good or bad until it is labeled as such in a person's mind. While most *good* people don't directly choose what happens to them, they choose their reaction to what happens to them. They choose to decide whether something is *good* or *bad* in their life by their interpretation of it. In fact, where these *good* people are today is the direct result of the choices these *good* people made yesterday. A person doesn't just wake up one day at the finish line. Some people look at their lives and wonder how they got where they are. The truth is that they <u>chose</u> to be where they are. Your life now is the sum total of all your past choices—good or bad. Since you can't change the past, you can't even wish for a fairer or better past. Just know that no one's past has been perfect. In fact, there is no *past perfect* tense in life. The past just was and lives where it should be—in the past! Let go of your hopes for a perfect past, and learn from the past that you did have. All you can really do is to make good decisions in the present, which will affect your future. You can't change yesterday, but you sure can ruin today by worrying about tomorrow.

Your history is nothing to be ashamed of, but it may be something to walk away from. History is helpful, but only to learn from. You have to know who you were in order to know who you are, but also know that *who you were is not who you are*. Outside conditions do not determine who you are. I grew up poor. That's who I was, not who I am. After building a secure future once, I was made poor again by a departing ex. Again, that's who I was, not who I am. People live and act according to their personal truths—their beliefs about themselves. Being a victim was not consistent with who I was in my mind, so I had to mentally change clothes and dress myself as a victor. Once my self-image changed, my circumstances changed; and then my world changed. It was all because I changed my focus, and begun to think differently. You can too once you start to *visualize victory*. If you can imagine success, your subconscious will help you achieve it. However, in order to create a new future, you have to let go of the past; or you will just keep reliving it. Forgive the past, for your sake, so you can live in the present, or your past will just become an anchor around your neck.

In life, all kind of weather occurs; but some people see only raindrops because they're looking at life from the gutter. These people never look up to see a rainbow, because they're focusing so hard on the gutter. You can't have a *rainbow without the rain*, but you have to look for the rainbow and stop focusing on the rain. When you meet these unfortunate people who only seem to look down, teach them how to look up and to change their focus. Don't go *grubbing in the garden of gloom* with these *les miserables*! Instead, help others not to cultivate a garden of gloom and doom, but to change their lives by looking up. We are constantly creating our lives by what we focus on. When you focus on what you don't want, a lack of something, or all the problems in your life, you are creating more of those. If you really want to create more problems in your life, just keep focusing on your current problems. You will find that is exactly what you are creating—more problems. Wow! If you are that powerful, why not focus on what you really do want in your life, like joy, happiness, or fulfillment, and then create those things? Cancel all negative thoughts and connect with what you want to create. Put a big red stop sign over negatives in your life. Create just the opposite by focusing only on positives.

Helen Keller once said, "*When one door of happiness closes, another opens; but often, we look so long at the closed door that we do not see the one that has been opened for us.*" Our future all depends on what we are focusing on and what we are looking for. Don't look for something without expecting to find it. If the results in your life are not what you want them to be, realize that they are what your current thinking has created for you. On the other hand, you can change your life just by changing your mind. Even if you are going through the darkest of days, remember God doesn't bring us *to* something without showing us the way *through* something. Just look for the rainbow on any cloudy day and let your thoughts about the rainbow chase the clouds away.

When you go outside, immediately look up; and you will see the blue sky, the stars, the moon, a sunset, a sunrise, perhaps even a rainbow, or many other magnificent things that will make you happy. If you look down, you will see the cold, hard pavement, the mud, the ants, the worms, the spiders, and all the creepy, crawly creatures that are certainly there. What would you rather choose to focus on? When you go outside, look up and think of all the infinite possibilities in the universe. God paints a different picture in the sky every day. Look up at the *pie in the sky*, and then look straight ahead as you decide where you would like your destination to be. Never look down because you will focus on the ants or the dirt. Look up, and things in your life will start to look up! Your future can actually be foretold by where you choose to place your face and your focus. When you focus on *blue skies* and happiness in the moment, then you will have a happy life, moment by moment. Thank God we don't have to count our moments, but we do have to make each moment count!

There was a movie entitled *Tender Mercies*, which contained a message about life. The movie's message was that you can't trust happiness. The moment the main character in this movie would allow himself to be happy about something, that happiness was snatched away from him, as if by some jealous gods. The real message of the movie should have been that you can't trust happiness when you put someone else in charge of your happiness, since you can't control what another person might do. However, you can trust happiness when you create it on your own. If you allow your happiness to be dependent on another person, place, or thing, it is not within your control, and therefore can be fleeting. When you are self-employed as your own *happiness boss*, no one can take your happiness away from you. Since you created your happiness in the first place, it means that you can recreate it anytime you wish. True security comes from knowing that you are in control of your own happiness, because it is generated from within.

If money could buy happiness, the richest people in the world would be the happiest; but that is not the case. Many millionaires seldom even smile. If you let your happiness be dependent on your wealth, remember that wealth can be fleeting, and can fluctuate up and down.

Most people look for a *reason* to be happy. Why does one need a reason to be happy? Happy just *is*! Thank God you don't have a reason to be unhappy, which is more of an unnatural state. The happiest people in the world are the ones who just make up their minds to be happy, knowing that they are in charge of their own minds! Happiness resides inside. It is actually just a journey *home. Call home!*

Happiness doesn't have to be deserved or earned. You can't work for happiness since it's free! It is just there inside of you waiting to be tapped. Happiness is like a gold mine inside of you just waiting to be mined once you discover the value of this precious metal. No one but you can tap the gold mine that is inside of you, although you can decide to give the gold away once you have mined it. The mine never dries up. Your happiness is your gift to the world, so keep mining it and giving it away freely.

Go back inside to where your joy resides. Wouldn't it be better to believe in a concept of *original joy*, which we were all born with, instead of a concept of *original sin? Joy* is just allowing yourself to feel what is inside of you and to share it with others. *Sin* is when you knowingly hurt another person. We were not born to be *sinners*, we were born to be *Joyners!* Enjoy your life! To enjoy, means to **enter into joy.** Once you have created joy in your life, entertain joy; and it will keep coming back! Create a favorite place in your mind that brings you comfort—a place that you can go to anytime you want, where just joy exists. Make this your *exist strategy* when the world is wearing you down. Life is about living, but don't be so busy making a living that you forget to make a life!

Happiness is the state that everyone should want to live in. When you live in the state of happiness, you will do certain things just because you are happy and not to make yourself happy. After all, happiness is where you come from when you are a *Happean.* Instead of trying to get there, start from there. Know that it is your core, your essence to be there. No one has to bring you to happiness. You were born there! Another person may choose to live there with you by living in the same state as you, but that person cannot make you move or take credit for where you were born.

Since happiness is a choice. Ask yourself, *"What is my happiness quotient (HQ) on a scale of 1 to 10? What could make my HQ higher?"* Why not make your headquarters (H.Q.) where your happiness quotient is the highest? Happiness radiates. Just like dropping a stone in a pond, concentric circles will radiate out from the point of entry and form a ripple effect spreading happiness everywhere.

One day while I was soaking in my whirlpool and reflecting on this concept of happiness, I noticed a bluebird sitting in a barren tree outside my window. I dubbed this bird the *bluebird of happiness* because it was in my own back yard. The bird reminded me of a play by Gerthe entitled *The Bluebird of Happiness.* The play was about two young children, who were out playing in their back yard, when one day, they spotted and were enticed by a bluebird. Thinking that this bluebird would bring them happiness if they could only catch it, the children tried hard to do just that. However, as soon as the children would approach the bird, it would fly away to a spot a few feet in front of them. This enticed both the children even more until they became obsessed with grabbing the bluebird. The children continuously followed the bird, which was always one step ahead of them. They actually followed the bird's path for years and years through every major city in Europe thinking that if they could only catch the bird, it would ensure their happiness. Unfortunately though, the children did not enjoy the trip. Instead of focusing on where they were, they focused on the elusive bluebird, who was always just one step ahead of them—visible, but not viable!

The children's whole lives were spent chasing that bluebird and obsessing so much about the chase that they didn't enjoy any of it. Only the bird was enjoying its life because it got to go wherever it wanted to go. Finally, the bluebird got old, which forced it to slow down; and it actually allowed itself to be caught. When the pursuers were finally able to grasp the bird, they looked around at where they were for the first time since the chase began. Suddenly, the realization hit that they were actually back in the same back yard where they had started. However, when the two captors looked at each other, these former children discovered that they had grown old! Life had passed them by. Now that they were elderly, they realized that they did not know where their lives had gone. Being so intent on the chase, the children had forgotten what life was all about.

By recognizing where they were, the former children finally realized that they had given up their whole lives only to learn that the bluebird of happiness was actually to be found *in their own back yard*. They realized that this was a valuable lesson—a lesson that it had cost them their whole lives to learn. Was it worth it? Wouldn't it have been better if the children had sprinkled some birdseed when they were young and enticed the bluebird to come to them? If they had fed and appreciated that bluebird, it would have continuously come back to them. Perhaps then they would have been able to enjoy the bluebird, without the compulsive need to possess it!

Is your *bluebird of happiness* always one step beyond where you are? What will it take for you to catch up with it? *Hopefully, not your whole life! Ask yourself, "When am I going to decide to be happy?" Or better yet, "When am I going to let myself be happy?" If your answer is not right now, ask yourself, "what has to happen first?"* Why are you choosing to miss all the current moments of joy in your life? Happiness can seem elusive until we realize that it's right here inside of us and has been all along! It is not something we have to chase or try to possess. It is just something we have to enjoy and set free within us. Happiness does not involve a chase. It is *where we are!*

Stop looking for happiness *out there somewhere.* Happiness comes from within. It can only be tempered by your perception of what is happening *out there somewhere.* The grass is always greener on the other side of the fence— *until you get there!*

Joy is our birthright, but the path to finding it is seldom clear. Maybe we should have dropped breadcrumbs when we were children so we would know how to get back to our inner child and our innate joy inside. A baby takes pleasure in everything around it, even if it's only the smile on its mother's face. A baby smiles, gurgles, and coos at everything, especially bright colors. Why can't we keep this innate joy as a precious gift throughout our lifetimes? What does a baby (who is completely helpless and dependent) know that we don't know? Why do we postpone happiness as an adult when we didn't as a child? What lessons did we learn in our early lives that caused us to put our *happiness on hold?*

Why do adults just take a short vacation to *happily ever after* every now and then, but don't really believe that they can afford to live there? At least, knowing where *there* is is a start! Hopefully, we will choose to live *there* permanently as soon as we believe that we can. Where did we, as adults, learn that our happiness isn't as important as other things in our lives? Why is it that we put our happiness on the back burner? When we take our last breath, will we finally realize that it's not how many breaths we took that were important, but the moments that took our breaths away? Create more breathless moments in your life, the kind that memories are made of.

Recently, a song came out with a meaningful message. The message was *"Don't blink! A hundred years go quicker than you think!"* As each event of your life goes by, don't be caught with your eyes shut! Relish each moment, but ask yourself, *"Where do I grow from here?"*

Take delight in each day as you design it; but while you are designing your life, take time to discover your purpose, which is what gives your life meaning. We all have a higher purpose or contribution to make to the universe and are given the talents or gifts that it will take to accomplish that purpose. Your life is a work of art that you are creating each day. Each moment is a brush stroke. Each moment can be an opportunity to create joy. How do you find your purpose? Find your joy. Find out what really makes you happy. Then go in that direction. Joy is a vibration. Rev up your receiver to the right frequency, so that joy can reverberate in your ears.

According to the Mayan calendar, the end of the world will occur December 21, 2012. Nostradamus and the *I Ching* have also predicted an apocalypse around the same time. Now all of their predictions just might signify that we will be entering a portal into a golden age, but if you were to believe that the world was going to end in less than a year, how would your behavior change? Would you not be making the most of each day? At best, if the average lifespan of a human is seventy-eight years, or 28,478 days, do we have a day to waste?

Are you loving to live and living to love each day? If not, what is stopping you? Who is stopping you from being you? Could it be that you're only unhappy because you don't know you're happy? When your head, your heart, and your gut all become connected, you will be feeling your passion.

Try doing less so that you can *feel* more. Engage in activities that let you combine your head with your heart. Give yourself permission to explore, but learn to be at peace with yourself. When you are feeling stressed, you will make a decision from your head about the things that really have to do with your heart.

The essence of your life should be about letting your vibrational frequency be in tune with your desires. Instead of swimming upstream against the current, sometimes all you need to do is to let go, float, and let your life be buoyed up and swept away by the current of source energy. Instead of resisting, turn and go with the flow, trusting the universe to take you in the right direction.

Voltaire once said, *"Paradise is where I am."* Since paradise is really inside of you, it can be no other place than where you are!

On our very first birthday ever, there was no cake, no candles, and no silly hats. We just showed up and were handed a great big beautiful gift called *life*. Your life is a gift—undeserved and unearned. What you do with your life is your gift in return!

What are you doing with this gift that is so precious and priceless? There is nothing that is worth more than your life! Are you letting it seep away moment by moment? Or are you spending each day in *You-phoria*, feasting at the buffet of life?

Each moment is precious, but *each moment is like holding a snowflake in your hand to admire its beauty until it is no more.* No two snowflakes are ever alike, just as each moment is precious and unique.

There are no *rollover minutes* in real life. Whether you use them or not, the minutes expire and are gone. All you can do is to make the most of your minutes by making each moment memorable.

The world needs *dreamers* and the world needs *doers;* but most of all, the world needs *dreamers who do.* I hope that is each and every one of you!

Remember, *awesome* begins with *awe* and ends with *me!* Make your *me* meaningful!

Today is the first day of the rest of your life! What are you going to do today that will make a difference in your life?

"Hello, this is your life calling......

Is anybody there?

Hello....."

CPSIA information can be obtained at www.ICGtesting.com
Printed in the USA
BVOW020019310112

281751BV00001B/10/P

9 781452 091853